Maximilian

EMPEROR OF

MEXICO

Memoirs of his Private Secretary

JOSÉ LUIS BLASIO

TRANSLATED FROM THE ORIGINAL SPANISH

AND EDITED BY

ROBERT HAMMOND MURRAY

FOREWORD BY CARLETON BEALS

NEW HAVEN

YALE UNIVERSITY PRESS

1934

Foreword

In his youthful memoirs Maximilian tells how he stood at the foot of the Royal Stairs in the Palace of Caserta and dreamed of unsheathing a golden sword to conquer a throne for himself. Not he but Marshals Forey and Bazaine at the head of the legionaries of Napoleon III transitorily rolled a republic into the dust and placed the ambitious Hapsburg Archduke upon the cactus throne of Mexico.

Maximilian's early writings reveal an adolescent romantic mind, engrossed in petty happiness and false dreams of grandeur. A Liberal Catholic, a parliamentary monarchist, a sentimental rationalist, his thought is shot through with borrowed French revolutionary sophistry. He presents us with a series of maxims on how the enlightened prince should govern, all of which he was to violate during his brief elevation to power—once more proving that philosophers may be kings but kings can rarely be philosophers. His brief rule in Mexico stands devastatingly condemned by his own youthful yardstick of idealism.

Maximilian and Carlota came to Mexico as sovereigns in 1864. They were disappointed at the squalor of Vera Cruz and the inadequacy of their reception. Their carriage became mired on the trip to the capital, and droll gossip has it that the first night there, the new Emperor slept on a billiard table because of the animation of the palace bed.

But their spirits were soothed by the triumphant floral arches, the smart French cavalry escort of "red legs," and the joyous *Te Deums* of the priests. Blithely Maximilian sat down on the Mexican volcano to write or have written a 600-page book of court etiquette. When still in Miramar, his Adriatic palace, even before he had accepted the throne, the youthful Archduke had sent off to Paris and London for samples of cloth and buttons for the liveries of his servitors. He promenaded through the following three years in a daze of glory, difficulties, self-righteous statesmanship, and glittering illusions.

The ephemeral empire set up for them by Napoleon collapsed in 1867. On the bright sunny morning of June 19 Maximilian fell before a firing squad on the Hill of Bells in Querétaro; Carlota had already gone raving mad in the Vatican and lingered on insane until her death in 1926. Napoleon's prestige was shattered. France was left disgraced, weakened; soon after, the country got a taste of what had been done to Mexico when the Prussian military heel was ground into its prostrate neck. But the Paris commune paid an unconscious debt to Mexico when it put the Swiss banker Jecker, whose intriguing had done so much to promote intervention in Mexico, against the executioner's wall. Blood-soaked Mexico itself was sunk in financial, economic, and political ruins. Maximilian's empire was built on blood, sand, and childish folly.

The bibliography of that tragic drama is staggeringly voluminous. If every soldier of Napoleon I carried a marshal's baton in his knapsack, apparently every literate soldier of Napoleon III carried an unpublished manuscript of memoirs. One Gallic critic declared that the French soldiers covered six thousand leagues, but brought back only the dust on their boots; certainly to judge by most of the accounts they wrote, they brought back little in their heads. Those copious contemporary records swelled into a flood of secondary works, particularly in French, German, and Spanish. But the first comprehensive study had to wait until 1928 when Count Corti brought out his excellent two-volume work.

Strangely enough the best first-hand account of the intimate life of Maximilian, that by his private secretary José Luis Blasio, was not published until 1905. Unavailable to earlier historians, it has been little utilized even by later students. A rare book, even in Spanish, until the present translation and editing by Robert Hammond Murray, it has never appeared in any other language.

The only similar personal document is that of Dr. Samuel Basch, the Emperor's surgeon for less than a year. He is constantly cited, probably because his book was published immediately after Maximilian's execution when public interest in the tragic imperial adventure was general throughout Europe.

But Blasio is a far more important source than Basch. Blasio became the Emperor's secretary a few months after the arrival of the sovereigns. He was an eye-witness of their triumphal entry into the capital; he portrays vividly the kaleidoscopic scenes that followed. Much favored, he scarcely left the Emperor's side from early morning until late at night; he accompanied him on all his junkets; he was present at nearly every state banquet as well as more intimate suppers. He was with the Emperor as the *régime* began to disintegrate under the blows of the Juárez armies and Napoleon III's betrayal.

Sent in 1866 on a special commission to Miramar, Blasio traveled to Rome with Carlota, who had frantically and fruitlessly hurried from Mexico to Paris to seek aid from Napoleon and then entreated it from the Vatican as a final desperate and vain resort. Graphically Blasio describes the accumulating disquieting symptoms—her growing persecution complex, which culminated in stark madness in the presence of the Pope.

Blasio hastened back to Mexico in time to endure the prolonged Querétaro siege with its black days of starvation, treachery, and disillusionment. To him and Basch the Emperor intrusted his most intimate personal papers to be burned.

After the execution, Blasio went back to Europe to carry out several thankless commissions for the dead monarch, saw his brother, Emperor Franz Joseph, his mother and other relatives, and peered sadly through the iron fence at the demented Carlota pacing under the trees of the Château of Laeken, near Brussels.

He did not whip his notes into final book form until thirty years ago. Its publication went practically unnoticed. The author, like most of Maximilian's followers, had already fallen on miserable days. He died in poverty and neglect in 1923 in a suburb of Mexico City.

His book covers the intimate side of Maximilian's life in Mexico; he had an inside view of all the most dramatic occurrences from the days of glittering prosperity to inevitable collapse. In the appendix Mr. Murray has wisely included those parts of the memoirs of the American ex-circus rider, Princess Salm-Salm, which detail her efforts to free Maximilian from his prison in Querétaro by bribing his custodians. Legend is that she offered more intimate and interesting gages than money, which last, alas, neither she nor Maximilian had. The account by the dashing unprincipled lady fills a brief gap in Blasio's story with an equally vivid first-hand chronicle.

Blasio is a gossipy raconteur. He tells of the clothes the Emperor and Empress wore, the dishes they ate, the wines they drank, the people they met. Wholly worshipful of the sovereign, Blasio found no detail too simple to record. This very Boswellian *naïveté* and lack of critical comprehension enhance the value of his observations.

Not only does the book cover Maximilian's rule in
Mexico, but it completes the psychological record that
Maximilian left broken when he turned from memoirs to
action and attempted to put the dreams and maxims of his
youth into practice. Blasio's excellent powers of observation, his earnest desire to portray faithfully, illuminate
those personal motives and abilities which so influenced the
historical events. The emperor's gaiety, spontaneous and
forced, his petty vanities, his noble and generous impulses,
his flashes of cowardice and courage, his rationalism and
his superstitions, his weaknesses and stubbornness, his secret love-affairs, his kindliness, his genial snobbery, his
pampered self-indulgences and bursts of martial energy—
all the rainbow visions of his soap-bubble world are there,
from the days when he shivered from the upland chill in his
dismal overheated palace apartments to the days when he
galloped over the plains with aching heart and mortal
fears. Now he goes gaily off to Cuernavaca behind his
twelve spanking snow-white mules, light-hearted as a child
on a holiday. Now—according to another chronicler—he
is weeping in the Chapultepec gardens, still very much a
child, in the midst of the crumbling ruins of his dream. And
finally, too late, desperate over the fate of Carlota, trapped
in an impossible situation, he bravely seizes the golden
sword in a last foolish attempt to save his throne.

Maximilian is one of the great protagonists of historical
pathos, and Blasio's account is a very human document;
it reveals a weak man sustained by a constant sense of nobility and self-righteousness.

Maximilian never knew much about Mexico, never
learned enough Spanish fully to understand his inquisi-
tors during hearings outside the court at Querétaro for
the trial that spelled his doom and which he was too ill to
attend. But he was sincere and had wished to do well by his

chosen fatherland; on his death he prayed that his might be the last blood spilled in Mexico. Vain hope.

Maximilian was a lamb among wolves. He was constantly wounded by the brusque realism and cynical crookedness of Marshal Bazaine and the harsh determination of Napoleon to make Mexico pay through the nose on the French debt. An enlightened Catholic, he was horrified at the narrow bigotry and greed of Archbishop Labastida and other Mexican prelates. He was equally horrified at the bloodthirstiness and predaciousness of his Mexican generals and cabinet members. He was shocked by the harsh treatment of the Indians and the universal denial of all the customary rights of man as he had learned them in his copious readings of French revolutionary thought. Maximilian's academic loftiness of purpose and his vacillations brought about a break with the French; he broke with Napoleon; he broke with the Church; he broke with the Mexican Conservatives. His own unshakable idealism and honesty caused him to fall into the abyss between all parties, so that those who remained by his side, with the exception of Miramón and the Indian Catholic Mejía, were mostly cheap adventurers, avaricious self-seekers, petty plotters, traitors.

Maximilian and Juárez were the noblest characters in the whole sordid mess of the intervention. Vaguely, even in his overweening self-superiority, Maximilian realized that the man he had come to depose and whose doctrines as set forth to him in Europe had seemed so iniquitous, was the key to the situation, though he never once had an inkling of the real driving genius of his Indian opponent or the inevitableness of the principles he espoused. He even indulged in the pipe-dream of an alliance with Juárez, the latter in a subordinate rôle of course, and engagingly sent him his autographed picture; but when the doughty Republican Indian scornfully repulsed his advances, Maximilian's childish spleen caused him to bow to Bazaine's suggestion that he sign the "Black Decree" which condemned every captured Mexican patriot to death. And yet before the end of his rule—and this has been ignored by historians—he had embodied in his decrees practically all the Juárez religious reforms he had come to oppose: such was the tide of new ideas and political forces upon which he was inevitably carried.

But he never really woke from his dreams. Even in the dark hour of his doom, trapped in the Querétaro death hole like a rat, he spent time in revising the rules of court etiquette; he asked the bloody and treacherous General Márquez (who broke through the iron ring of the Republican besiegers) to bring back with him, besides reinforcements, piano sheet music and other fripperies. Márquez never returned.

If precisely all these details are not found in Blasio, others equally amusing, significant, and intimate give us the clue to the greatest of nineteenth-century Don Quixotes. Besides Maximilian, other important and fantastic characters flash through the pages, all those who worked and strutted, plotted and played in the tinseled, meretricious and fleeting radiance of the marionette Emperor's court. What a puppet show it was! How well Blasio depicts it, while all the time—even to the belated day of the publishing of his memoirs nearly four decades later—he mused over and relived his rôle on the painted stage that he believed firmly was real; even then he seems still to have been unable to understand that gigantic failure!

The historical value of Blasio's account is obvious and thanks and credit are due Mr. Murray for rescuing it from undeserved oblivion and presenting it to us in his graphic and admirable translation, with appendix and notes. But as the one star in Blasio's firmament is Maximilian, and the chronicler is too dazzled to see anything else, the complicated financial, economic, political forces involved are not delineated. For the basic motives of the intervention, the reasons for the failure of the Empire, the dire consequences of that madcap adventure both to France and to Mexico, one must look elsewhere.

Among other things, the intervention was a definite attempt to test the strength of the Monroe Doctrine. Napoleon III was determined to revindicate Europe's right to meddle in New World affairs, and he seized the most opportune moment for such a test—the years when our Union was wholly absorbed in the life and death struggle of the Civil War. Napoleon, who clearly foresaw the great future strength and prosperity of the United States unless our development were curbed and our Latin American markets withheld from us, gave secret instructions to Forey and other representatives to oppose us at every step, to put up a bar to our further commercial and political expansion. He not only desired a well-situated foothold for France in the New World, but hoped that the setting up of a petty French Manchukuo in Mexico would strike a mortal blow at the further spread of democratic and republican principles.

Napoleon failed. Seward's ultimatums for immediate withdrawal of French troops, and later Juárez' implacability with regard to Maximilian's execution, wrote finis upon any attempted repetition of such an adventure. Napoleon's blunder strengthened the sovereignty of the Latin American states and promoted faith in popular government everywhere.

The French intervention is also very valuable as a case study of financial imperialism: the use of armed intervention to help international bankers collect debts and obtain unworthy concessions. Our past coercions in Cuba, Nicaragua, Colombia, Panama and elsewhere had their prototype in the Napoleonic intervention—especially in its financial aspects—save that the French were greedier, more ruthless, far more unrealistic. But three quarters of a century ago the French proclamations stressed the same catchwords of sanitation, law and order, and efficiency. If Marshal Forey could not, being a representative of an imperial sovereign, stress democracy, he did emphasize the popular benefits of military paternalism. All the wordy French manifestoes to the Mexican people portrayed France as the embodiment of "the ideals of the enlightened nineteenth century"—a phrase that echoes and reëchoes above the din of brutal battle and the dull roll of musketry shooting prisoners against deep-gouged blood-spattered adobe walls.

In reality those gilt-edge phrases hypocritically concealed the brutal ultimatum sent to Juárez to meet immediately all the French claims in full, claims which expanded with tropical exuberance to astonishing proportions. Such righteous phraseology concealed Jecker's spider-like machinations in conjunction with the Duc de Morny (a bastard brother of Napoleon), a force in French politics and at court. Mexican securities were liberally distributed among an influential court clique; and De Morny's close friend, Saligny, French Minister in Mexico (also personally involved in these shady financial deals), vigorously harassed the Juárez government with petty claims of allegedly injured Frenchmen, some of whom, it was later proven, did not even exist. Jecker and his group of Bourse gamblers sought to reward themselves at Mexico's expense and hoped for future windfalls in the subsequent financing of the new puppet state—all the eternal cynicism of private high finance in international affairs was in evidence, with the same willingness to grasp profits by war, blood-shed and national betrayal, while politicians and army offi-cers enunciate lofty purposes.

The story is all there: the corruption of high French government officials, the wangling of concessions, the false padding of debts, the insistence upon improper claims. In-deed, the account reads far worse, far more luridly than the four-volume report of the fairly recent Senate investiga-tions of our own foreign loans.

The most casual perusal of the Mexican year book of the time would have told the French that they would never collect from the Mexican people, though they seized the entire Mexican revenues for decades, even the interest on their fantastic claims, let alone any of the principal. What happened, of course, as usually happens in such imperial-istic adventures, was that Mexico was ruined and the French people themselves paid heavily in order that a small clique of court favorites and bankers might make hay while the sun shone. Bankers and politicians had their old worthless obligations made good by new loans totaling hun-dreds of millions of francs foisted upon the gullible French public, dazzled by the idea of brilliant conquest and the supposed honesty of their financial leaders supported by court friendship.

The third interventionist motive was religion. The Mexican constitution of 1857 destroyed medieval Church privileges, subjected priests to the civil law, separated Church and State, secularized cemeteries, provided for civil registry, confiscated Church properties, suppressed monasteries. This and Juárez' 1859 Reform Laws aroused great hostility among the Catholic powers of Europe. The Conservative pro-Church Mexican émigrés swarmed about the various courts and the Pope; they even pulled wires in England. They found sympathetic ears in Catholic Spain

and Austria; they were amiably received by Princess
Eugénie who wept over the sufferings of the Church in
Mexico as recounted to her by fat Archbishop Labastida;
and José Hidalgo, one of the most active conspirators,
found access to the ear of Napoleon through the boudoirs
of Eugénie and the Queen Mother. The Catholic powers
were determined to stamp out Mexican Jacobinism and
republicanism and restore all religious feudal rights.

Thus religion, profit, high finance, and imperial ambition locked arms to set up the monarchy in Mexico with
foreign bayonets, aided, it must be noted, by Mexicans
themselves, who for years had sought and entreated the
intervention. When it came, even many supposedly staunch
Republicans stampeded traitorously to climb on the imperial bandwagon and help betray the fatherland.

Mexico had begun its independence with a Catholic Emperor, the renegade royalist officer, Agustín Iturbide. But
he was soon swept aside by the ambitious independence generals, mouthing principles of democracy and republicanism. Though the antecedents of the Church struggle go
far back into the colonial period, independence acceler-
ated the effort to bring about Church-State separation and
other religious reforms. The first important "Liberal" victory came with the 1833 Gómez Farías Laws. But this anti-
clerical tendency was soon smothered by Conservative pro-
monarchist forces. From then on, the tide of civil war (its
purposes ever obscured by the fantastic volatile personality of the one-legged opportunist, Santa Ana) swept
higher, until the victory of Juan Alvarez and Ignacio
Comonfort. The resultant 1857 Reform constitution and
the 1859 Reform Laws provided the nation's legal basis—
save for the short-lived governments of Zuloaga, Miramón, and Maximilian—until the 1917 Querétaro constitution.

When Juárez suspended payment on the Mexican foreign debt, held by British, French, and Spanish interests, a pretext for intervention was provided. Through the cajoleries of Napoleon and the Mexican émigrés, a convention was signed in London in 1861, by which the three injured countries pledged themselves to support an armed attempt to force the Mexican government to meet its obligations. Though not signatories, Belgium and Austria promised aid.

Spain hastened to send the first expedition, a larger contingent than the one stipulated in the agreement, and was already in possession of Vera Cruz when the French and British forces arrived. The leaders of the three expeditions soon quarreled. England wished only her money and had no sympathy with the monarchical intrigues of Spain and France. Spain wished to impose on Mexico a Bourbon or one allied to that house; Napoleon desired a ruler chosen and controlled by him. His personal representative, General Lorencez, acted in a high-handed independent fashion; the French hastened to send over a force which would outnumber that of Spain.

British statesmen soon wormed out of the trap Napoleon had set for them; the British forces sailed away. When Napoleon's purpose to throw a large army into Mexico became increasingly apparent, the Spanish also withdrew. Soon after, England and Spain signed a satisfactory treaty with Juárez. Napoleon now had a free hand to act alone.

Lorencez, not at all realizing he was dealing with veterans of years of civil warfare, had utter contempt for Mexican courage and equipment. At the gates of Puebla he hurled his 5,000 troops against the hill-perched battlements of the forts of Guadalupe and Loreto—a stupid Bunker Hill tactic. His forces cut to pieces and utterly routed, he fled back to Orizaba. With more initiative the

Mexicans could easily have completely annihilated the entire French expedition.

Lorencez' terrible reverse was the first grave blow to Napoleon's prestige. French national pride was aroused; the Emperor was obliged to remove the blot of that defeat from the Empire's escutcheon. It took the French a year to get their feet under them and begin a real advance into the interior. By then 25,000 more troops were ashore at Vera Cruz, commanded by General Forey, a French politician who issued proclamations so copiously that he had to be reprimanded by Napoleon. Even so it required two months of terrific siege and bloody fighting to overpower the courageous defenders of Puebla.

With its fall, the road to Mexico City was open. Juárez removed his government to Querétaro, then was driven from pillar to post, and finally pushed to the border. But using what is now Ciudad Juárez as a base, the Republicans gradually reconquered their country with the puissant aid of the United States.

The French had established a provisional government of thirty-five "Notables," handpicked by intriguing French Minister Saligny, a bloc to be the nucleus of an Assembly of 215 members, theoretically representing the whole people of Mexico. Many were so shabby they had to be provided with clothes by the French army. An Oaxaca newspaper observed that of the delegates "representing" that state, only one had ever been heard of before.

The Notables promptly leapt through the tissue loop. They decreed the adoption of a constitutional monarchy and decided to offer the crown of Emperor to Archduke Maximilian, brother of Franz Joseph, or if he declined, to some other Catholic prince. A provisional government was vested in the triumvirate of General Almonte, General Salas, and Archbishop Labastida. A commission proceeded to Miramar to offer Maximilian the throne in the name of the "Notables."

Carlota was dazzled by the prospect. But eager as was Maximilian, although he was chafing in idleness and thought he wanted a job and a throne, he hesitated; he demanded adequate financial and military support from France and a plebiscite. The French army proceeded to collect the votes. How quickly it learned to imitate the system that largely endures to this day for the inducting of so-called democratic presidents into office! Puppet officials imposed upon subjugated regions merely sent in word under due seal and flourish that so many people in their jurisdiction had voted for Maximilian. One voting place was actually set up in Mexico City, and every passer-by was rounded up by attendant soldiers and forced to sign his acquiescence. The "returns" gave Maximilian an overwhelming majority. There is no reason to disbelieve that, in his ingenuousness and complete ignorance of what was going on in Mexico, he really imagined that the Mexican people had "voted" him the crown.

With due ceremony the Mexican flag was run up over Miramar castle. Maximilian and Carlota set forth for Rome to receive the blessing of the Pope, and then sailed for Mexico—in the same Austrian cruiser that later bore the Emperor's bullet-riddled body back to Europe. We next see them passing under a triumphal arch to enter Mexico City.

At this point the curtain rings up on the second act of the tragedy. From here on Blasio's book carries us to the grim and sanguinary finale.

CARLETON BEALS

Mexico City.

CONTENTS

APPENDICES

NOTES

INDEX

LIST OF ILLUSTRATIONS

PART I

𝕿𝖍𝖊 𝕮𝖔𝖚𝖗𝖙

1864-1865

THOSE residents of Mexico City and of Guadalupe who are still living cannot forget June 11, 1864, the day on which the Emperor Maximilian and the Empress Carlota made their triumphal approach to the capital.

From the early morning hours the plain of Aragón had presented a festive appearance. There were hundreds of open carriages filled with the most distinguished and beautiful women of Mexican society, escorted by men in formal attire. Under the clear blue skies crowds milled about carrying tricolored banners, leafy branches, and countless bouquets of gay flowers. It was a wonderful scene never to be forgotten by those who saw it, as I did.

When Maximilian and his wife made their appearance the enthusiasm of the throng broke out in frenzy. In the midst of a tumult of vivas a committee of the ranking men and women of Mexico City welcomed Maximilian and Carlota in the name of the inhabitants of the capital of the Empire. This was followed by a high mass in the church of Guadalupe. Later a banquet was served after which Their Majesties retired to rest before their entry into the city proper on the following day.

On June 12, the principal streets of the city appeared more like the halls of a great palace with triumphal arches made of flowers, enormous mirrors, carpeted walks, and Mexican and foreign flags. In the vanguard of His Majesty's retinue came the regiment of Mexican lancers under the command of Colonel López. After them rode the French regiment of the Chasseurs of Africa and the Hussars preceding the state coach. On both sides of Their Majesties, riding on magnificent horses, were Generals Bazaine and Neigre escorted by their staffs; sixty coaches occupied by dignitaries of the Empire followed the imperial carriage. The sovereigns went first to the cathedral where a solemn *Te Deum* was chanted, and after this ceremony they walked to the palace in the midst of a multitude of more than a hundred thousand persons who filled the air with their deafening applause.

It was then, almost within touching distance of him, that I could for the first time look closely at the man to whom later I should become debtor for countless benefits. I saw him pass, arrogant, majestic, and well proportioned. Above all I was impressed by the mildness of his expression which later it was my privilege to contemplate so many times. His long golden beard, parted in the center, gave him such an aspect of majesty that it was impossible to see him without immediately being attracted and fascinated.[1]

Some days afterwards my mother received a letter informing her that my brother, who was only fifteen years old and who a few months before had left his home to join the revolutionists [Liberals], was a prisoner in the Martinica, named after the street in which it stood. He had been captured by the French who were pursuing the guerrilla band led by Nicolás Romero, with whom he had taken the field, and was in danger of being executed. My mother appealed to some old friends of my father, some of whom signed a petition to the Emperor, asking him to pardon the boy because of his age. Taking the petition with us, one morning my mother and I went to Chapultepec, where the sovereigns were in residence. In company with many other petitioners we waited for them to come out.

Soon two outriders who preceded the French carriage in

which Maximilian and Carlota rode trotted into sight. The vehicle halted in front of the group of petitioners. The Emperor, after courteously saluting everyone, took the papers that were handed him and placed them on the seat in front of him.

The Emperor that morning wore a long black cloak. From his neck hung the Order of the Golden Fleece, attached to a broad moire ribbon. Carlota's gown was of lilac silk. Covering her shoulders was a rich mantle of black silk. Her hat was also black. The Emperor wore a tall gray hat, of a pattern which soon became fashionable among the well-dressed men of the capital.

A few days later my brother came home. Thus my family contracted the first debt of gratitude to the generous and magnanimous man who three years later was to perish so tragically.

A friend of ours was on very good terms with officers of the French army, and one morning he informed me that a Belgian official, Robert Limelette Vanderlynden, who had a post in the office of the Emperor's secretary, had asked him if he knew anyone who understood French and was qualified to act as interpreter to Don Félix Eloin, Maximilian's secretary and advisor, who did not know a word of Spanish. I went to the palace, where Vanderlynden presented me to Eloin.

Eloin was a tall, heavy man of about fifty, serious and taciturn. Long mustaches fell to either side of his lips. He first impressed me as being stern and sour, but after exchanging a few words with him my opinion changed, for his agreeable although terse phrases, when I had dealt with him a little, showed me immediately that he was a man of the world and versed in the usages of polite society. He was, as I have said, a Belgian and by profession an engineer. He enjoyed limitless influence with the Emperor. No one knew why, but the fact remained that, having been recommended to Maximilian by his father-in-law, the King of the Belgians, he had attained an extraordinary ascendancy over the Emperor's mind.[2]

Having satisfied himself by a long conversation with me in French that I had sufficient command of the language, he handed me several letters in Spanish to translate into French, and I was immediately taken into his service. My duties consisted in acting as interpreter between Eloin and persons who did not speak French, in translating letters, and sealing correspondence for the Mexican ministers abroad.

My first meeting with the Emperor took place a few days after I had begun to work with Eloin. I was busy when His Majesty came into the office. He had walked up the spiral stairs from the ground floor of the palace to the room where I was working, on the first floor of the left wing. The Emperor that morning wore the uniform of a Mexican general, a blue cape with gilt buttons, blue riding breeches, and heavy boots. The Fleece was about his neck, hanging by a black ribbon.

Then for the first time I could scrutinize his face to my full satisfaction—the kindly glance of his blue eyes, his long blonde beard, and the drooping lower lip characteristic of the Hapsburgs. After talking briefly with me, he spoke to Eloin and then retired to his apartments.

Eloin a short time after this was sent to Europe on a mission. This was merely a pretext to remove him from the court, for he worked against the interests of the French, who intrigued to get rid of him. He was succeeded by Commandant Loysel and then by Captain Pierron.

During this period the Emperor, who profoundly disliked the climate of the capital, had gone to Orizaba [in the state of Vera Cruz] to be present at the wedding of his

friend, Naval Lieutenant Carlos Shaffer, to a Señorita
Bringas. Shaffer had accompanied the Emperor on his
voyage around the world; to this was due the high honor
that Maximilian bestowed upon him through his affection
and friendship.

A few days after the wedding the Emperor took up his
residence on the hacienda of Jalapilla, three miles from
Orizaba, and from there he ordered Loysel to send him
some documents, by courier and not by post, for fear that
they might be stolen. Loysel honored me by choosing me to
take the documents to Maximilian. I started for Orizaba
in a stagecoach, well escorted, with the papers for which
the Emperor had asked.

Two days later, in the midst of darkness and torrential
rain, at nine o'clock at night I arrived at Orizaba, and at
once presented myself to Colonel Feliciano Rodríguez, who
immediately provided a carriage to take me to Jalapilla.

When I reached the imperial residence, everything was
silent. About the house sentry duty was being performed
by the Austrian Hussars while the corridors were guarded
by men of the gigantic stature characteristic of the Palace
Guard.

I went to the quarters of the Emperor's private secretary, Nicholas von Poliakovitz, a young, jovial, attractive
Austrian, who spoke French, German, English, and Spanish perfectly. He told me to leave the papers with him, to
return to Orizaba to sleep, and to come the following day
to receive the Emperor's orders.

At the hour named by Poliakovitz, I was at the hacienda
and was immediately taken to the Emperor's room, a large
apartment, through the windows of which Maximilian
could see the high, blue mountains that surround Orizaba.
That morning Maximilian wore the white clothes which

he always adopted when he traveled in the tropics. He was seated at a table covered with papers, and on which lay his finely woven Panama hat, with a gold cord. The furnishings of the room consisted of several cane chairs, a dressing table, a washstand and a narrow iron bedstead, which he always used in his travels, for he never slept in the sumptuous beds which were prepared for him.

"How did you find your journey?" he asked pleasantly. "Is it the first time you have left Mexico City? How do you like this climate? I find it charming; I prefer it a thousand times to the debilitating and unhealthy air of the capital." Then he added: "You may remain here for a few days and return to your office later. I have ordered a room prepared for you, and tell me if there is anything I can offer you."

A servant showed me to my room and a few minutes afterwards I was summoned to breakfast, for during his journeys the Emperor proscribed palace etiquette, and about his table were seated all the members of his escort. The meal that day was served on one of the wide verandas, on dishes which bore the Emperor's monogram and the imperial crest.

His Majesty sat at the center of the table, with the Foreign Minister, Don Fernando Ramírez, at his right. At his left was the Minister of *Fomento*,* Don Luis Robles. Adjoining the two ministers were Colonel Feliciano Rodríguez, the aide-de-camp, and Colonel Paulino Lamadrid, who was in charge of the Emperor's horse, and in command of the mounted Municipal Guard.

Among the others were two adjutants, Pedro Ormaechea and Ciro Uraga; next to Uraga sat Colonel Miguel López,

---

* Literally, "encouragement" or "development"; corresponding more or less to the Secretary of Commerce and the Secretary of the Interior in the American president's cabinet.

one of the firmest supporters of the Emperor. López was of very light complexion, blonde with blue eyes, which caused many to believe that he was a Frenchman.

The remaining guests were Dr. Semeleder, the Emperor's physician, who had come from Europe in his service; the secretary, Poliakovitz; two Austrian officers of hussars, Count Pachta and Baron von Kulmer; Don Francisco O'Gorman, secretary to Minister Ramírez, and I.

Overseeing the waiters and the service was the majordomo, Venisch, an elderly man who had been with the Emperor for years, including the period when Maximilian was governing Venetian Lombardy. There were eight servants, Mexicans and foreigners.

His Imperial Majesty was a refined gastronome and his cooks did their best not to disappoint him. The cuisine was French, modified to some extent by the culinary art of Vienna. The finest wines were served at the imperial table; at breakfast sherry, bordeaux, burgundy, and wine of Hungary; at dinner Rhine wine and champagne, as well as those mentioned before.

During his meals the Emperor enjoyed listening to piquant and daring stories, above all if they related to some of the guests. After coffee was served, he arose immediately, bowing to everyone, and retired to his apartments to work with some of his ministers or secretaries. At breakfast and dinner an orchestra played.

While I was at Jalapilla the Emperor awoke at four o'clock, rose and immediately summoned his secretary, with whom he worked until seven. He afterwards rode, accompanied by his aides and grooms. His mount was usually a gentle horse named Anteburro. He preferred a Mexican to an English saddle, and was elegantly garbed for riding in a charro suit of blue woolen cloth with silver ornaments and a wide gray sombrero with a white band. But for ceremonial occasions his horse was a magnificent spirited bay called Orispelo.

His Majesty returned from his ride at nine, and a few minutes later breakfast was served. He then received his ministers or secretaries, gave audiences to persons who solicited them or drove to Orizaba, where he visited by preference the schools, prisons, hospitals, and other public establishments, always taking with him someone to make notes of the most urgent necessities of these institutions.

Dinner was at four. At its end all passed into another room to smoke. The servants offered fine Havana and Mexican cigars, which were smoked standing, to the accompaniment of agreeable conversation. When the Emperor had finished his cigar he retired, saying a phrase which became proverbial: "I shall say farewell to the gentlemen."

Toward nightfall he took a brief walk in the garden, and then retired to his room to look over the papers and letters that had been received during the day. Punctually at eight o'clock his valets came to assist him to disrobe and he went to bed, to awake, as I have said, at four, for one of his rules of hygiene was that a man required eight hours' sleep in order to preserve his health and to insure long life.

At this time the Emperor employed me in making extracts from documents and in copying letters; or he called me to read papers to him and note his instructions on the margins. One morning he informed me that we were going to Jalapa, and added: "I believe that it will please you to accompany us, and I have already ordered that you be supplied with a good horse and a hundred pesos with which to buy yourself a proper charro suit."

In the early days at Jalapilla the Emperor had summoned the Minister of War, Don Juan de Dios Peza, and

Count von Thun, who commanded the Austrian Legion, to discuss with them the delicate question of reorganizing the Mexican army. After a series of conferences between the three, a letter was written to Bazaine, upon whom Napoleon III had just conferred a marshal's baton, manifesting Maximilian's desire that the count should be placed in charge of the army reorganization, for lack "of a Mexican or French general who cares to, or who can, assume the task."

These phrases hurt Bazaine profoundly, and the naming of Count von Thun increased the antagonism between the Austrians and the French, and created a serious obstacle to the reorganization.

We started for Jalapa on May 19, at five o'clock in the morning. Only Minister Ramírez and his secretary journeyed by carriage, by another road, as the Emperor did not wish to expose him to the fatigues and dangers of the trip on horseback through the mountains. We were lodged at Huatusco in the house of Don Clemente González, where a banquet of sixty covers was served. Such an elaborate array of viands was provided that the Emperor remarked that the loyal citizens of Huatusco, probably desiring to perpetuate the memory of his visit, sought to kill their guests by indigestion. The attractiveness of the town led the Emperor to remain there for three days. On leaving he wished to give one thousand pesos, to be devoted to the necessities of the place. To his surprise, the authorities declined to accept the money, saying that in Huatusco there were no needy people, for everyone worked and their earnings provided them with enough to live on. The Emperor insisted that his gift be retained to improve the hospital, inasmuch as he desired not to visit any locality without leaving some beneficent trace of his passing.

On entering Jalapa the Emperor's escort presented a dazzling appearance, for we had donned our gala dress and the army officers their most brilliant uniforms. The imposing figure of the Emperor was conspicuous among the rest, clad as he was in his rich charro suit and mounted upon his magnificent bay horse.

As in Orizaba and the places previously visited by the sovereign, his entry into Jalapa was a triumph, amounting almost to a frenzy. The vivas, the applause, the cries of enthusiasm, the triumphal arches, all induced belief in what was really true: that the mere presence of the Emperor was sufficient to win general sympathy to him.

Magnificent quarters for His Majesty had been prepared on the principal street. After a brief rest and breakfast, we went to the church to hear mass; at its conclusion the Emperor strolled through the streets, and in all of them became the object of fresh manifestations of the enthusiasm of the citizens. There was a dinner at five o'clock.

On the following day, in the morning, a solemn *Te Deum* was chanted in the cathedral. The Bishop of Jalapa received the Emperor at the entrance, under a canopy. Near the high altar was a throne, upholstered with golden embroidery, on which His Majesty took his seat, with Minister Ramírez on his right and Minister Robles on his left.

On the following days he visited schools, hospitals, and other public establishments and the beautiful wood of Coatepec, on his way to the village of the same name, where he was entertained at breakfast under the trees.

On one of these excursions the Emperor's secretary, Poliakovitz, was the victim of an accident, which led to my joining permanently the sovereign's personal secretarial staff. He sustained a fractured arm by being thrown from a spirited horse. The Emperor ordered me to take charge of all documents, letters, etc., including the ciphers used in communicating confidentially with the ministers in Mexico and abroad and with the members of the civil and the military cabinets. I also took from Poliakovitz' lodgings a valise containing insignia of the Orders of Guadalupe and of the Mexican Eagle; gold, silver and bronze medals of civil and military merit, and articles of jewelry, for the most part gold watches with covers enameled in blue, with the monogram of the Emperor and the imperial crest in small brilliants; rings and scarfpins, similarly enameled in blue, and with the imperial monogram. These were from the chancelleries of the two orders, and intended to be bestowed on persons the Emperor encountered on his journeys who he thought should be rewarded for good service or merit, notice being given to the chancelleries to issue the certificate accrediting the honor conceded by His Majesty to the recipient. The jewelry was obtained by the secretary from Señor von Kuhachevich, the Treasurer of the Imperial Household, an elderly man, very devoted, who had come to Mexico with Maximilian.

At four o'clock the next morning I was summoned by His Majesty. The Emperor's bedroom was lighted by candles placed on a work table. He wore a blue flannel dressing gown and chamois slippers. While I read documents and letters to him, some in French and others in Spanish, he took off the dressing gown and, standing in his shirt, washed his face and hands. His two valets, one an Italian of the name of Grill, who was very popular with all the servants, and the other an Austrian, arranged the Emperor's hair and beard and aided him to dress.

After drinking a small cup of coffee or chocolate and eating two or three Vienna biscuits, he walked about the room, listening attentively as I read and dictating his orders. Then he seated himself at the table to sign the letters which had been written the night before. Since his signature was very heavy and left a good deal of wet ink on the paper, the signed letters and documents were spread out on the table and, when this was covered, on the carpet of the room—because the sovereign disliked to use blotting paper.

When we had finished I gathered up all the papers and went to my room, to place the letters in envelopes, and the documents intended for the ministers in their respective portfolios, and get them ready for the morning post. Promptly at nine o'clock breakfast for two was served in the Emperor's room. From this day I joined him at the meal, at the palace as well as at Chapultepec. This high distinction had not been bestowed on previous secretaries and did not fail to earn for me the ill will of the courtiers, especially the foreigners, who were unable to tolerate the idea that a humble Mexican should have the honor of being the only person to breakfast with the Emperor.

We left Jalapa on June 2, at daybreak, being escorted by a large company of horsemen three or four leagues from the city. His Majesty entered his traveling coach and invited me to join him; I seated myself at his left, and began to read the papers we had with us and to note down his instructions. As he felt the cold very much, he wore a light gray topcoat, of which he was fond and which he used even while in prison at Querétaro. A felt hat, also of light gray, covered his head. As his hair was thin the cold affected his head most. On his knees was a heavy plaid, which spread over his legs and feet. He shared the plaid with me, saying that evidently I must suffer as much as he from the cold.

I acquired the habit of writing in the coach, during our many later trips, and it became as easy for me to write there as upon a table, even when we were going at full speed. The coach was a commodious coupé with two seats and a large compartment in front, where the major-domo had placed provisions and glasses for two and a bottle of wine.

When we had finished with the papers, the Emperor asked me if I noticed how the fresh air sharpened one's appetite. As we were not due at Perote until midday, he added: "I am hungry now, and you must be, too; let us give ourselves a pleasant surprise by eating something quietly." Reaching into the locker, he handed out the dishes and a napkin which contained a roast turkey, a piece of cheese, some cold meat in jelly, etc. These he shared with me and after emptying a glass of wine at a single draft passed the bottle to me and invited me to drink. When we had finished he wrapped the dishes and what was left of the food in the napkin and replaced them in the locker.

Through the windows of the coach the officers of the escort who were galloping on either side could see us breakfasting. "Poor fellows," the Emperor said to me, laughing, "we know how they are envying us, but we can't invite them."

Taking out a case of cigars, he lighted one and offered me another, which I did not accept. After smoking a little he quit the cigar and slept until he was awakened at the next post by the fireworks and cheers of the enthusiastic Indians.

In the evening [at Perote] the town was brilliantly illuminated and the Austrian soldiers entertained the Emperor with amateur theatricals. The performance was given in German, and as the female as well as the male parts were taken by men, it was ludicrous to see the tall and martial figures of the brawny veterans covered with women's clothes.

Very early on the morning of June 4 we left Perote, to

begin the difficult ascent over the summits of Acultzingo to
the central tableland. The Emperor made his triumphal
entry into Puebla at six minutes to nine in the morning;
it was his second visit to the city. After breakfasting,
Maximilian visited the rooms which had been prepared for
the Empress and manifested his satisfaction at seeing the
magnificent double bed, with its canopy of fine lace and
silken ribbons, which was waiting for the imperial pair.
But as soon as the host was out of the way His Majesty
ordered the servants to find a room at a distance from the
bedchamber and set up his traveling cot there. He did this
almost angrily.

Being completely new to the court, and not having confidence in any of the servants, I was unable to let any of
them know how strange Maximilian's conduct seemed to
me. What conjugal drama was concealed by the Emperor's
action? Why was it that two young married persons, who
in public seemed to love each other, at the age of vigor
shared no marital life, and the husband appeared irritated
at the prospect of sleeping in the same bed with his wife?

Later I was completely convinced that some estrangement existed between them, something the nature of which
for the moment I was unable to decide; whether it was
created because of reasons of state, because of the Emperor's infidelity or because of some organic defect in
Maximilian. For neither in Puebla, nor in Mexico City in
the palace, nor at Chapultepec did they ever sleep together. This could not escape the servants' notice, for the
attendants of the Empress slept near her and those of
Maximilian in a room adjoining his.

Could one for a moment suppose that this isolation was
voluntary, when they were mutually interested in found-
ing a dynasty, as well as a monarchy, in Mexico? Was
the Emperor, as some said, sterile, and had he for this

CARLOTA
IN 1866

MAXIMILIAN
IN 1866

reason agreed to make Prince Agustín Iturbide his heir?
That the alliance of Maximilian and Carlota was founded
on love and not reasons of state no one in Mexico doubted.
The Emperor's youth, his physique, his personal attractions caused one to suppose that as a bachelor he had been
the hero of many gallant adventures in his travels through
Greece and Asia Minor and afterwards around the world;
assurance of this was provided by reliable persons who
knew of Maximilian's life during his travels. After his
marriage his conduct had been irreproachable. But, nevertheless, if some slip on his part had reached the ears of his
wife, it can easily be believed that in her woman's pride—
and the pride of a beautiful woman—she would have refused to lead a connubial life with him, and that it was
only for the sake of social expediency that they appeared
before the world to be living in the greatest harmony.

As the hour approached for the Empress' arrival, Maxi-
milian drove to meet her at the entrance to Puebla from
Mexico City in a magnificent carriage, drawn by four
spirited horses, followed by his aides and adjutants. The
Empress was accompanied by a lady of honor, Señora
Pacheco, and Count von Bombelles, commander of the
Palace Guard, which escorted her. Her servants followed
in other carriages.

The Emperor descended from his coach and went to
that of the Empress. He entered it and clasped her hand
affectionately. In the midst of the frenzied enthusiasm of
the Puebla citizens, under triumphal arches and a con-
tinuous rain of flowers, the sovereigns for the second time
entered Puebla. When they had rested for a few minutes
dinner was served. They then went to the principal balcony of the episcopal palace to witness fireworks displayed
in their honor and to listen to an elaborate serenade by
military bands.

At sunrise on June 7 a salvo of artillery, the pealing of the bells in all the churches and the music of military bands marching through the streets joyfully announced the celebration of the birthday of the Empress of Mexico, the second she had spent in the country and, by a singular coincidence, also the second she had passed in Puebla. The year before she and the Emperor had halted in Puebla on their way from Vera Cruz to the capital. Then the ladies of Puebla offered Carlota a bouquet formed of the rarest and most exquisite flowers of the tropics, and the Empress gave from her private purse seven thousand pesos to restore the hospital, the ruinous aspect of which had pained her when she saw it.

On the second anniversary she spent in Puebla she gave new proofs of her munificence and her goodness. She asked the Emperor, as an act of grace, to liberate 235 prisoners of war, which he immediately ordered Count von Thun to do. Fifteen prisoners in the city jail were also released. Her Majesty on this day, from her private purse, presented one thousand pesos to the foundling asylum and to the hospital of San Pedro, five hundred to the sisters of San Vincente de Paul, one hundred to the Capuchin convent and three hundred to the poor.

A very attractive woman of Puebla, the wife of a wealthy merchant, was named [among others] by the Empress as a lady of honor; but she returned the notice, saying that she preferred to be queen in her own house and not a servant in the palace. Having been invited to the banquet and ball [in honor of the Empress] she attended, accompanied by her two beautiful daughters. She was received so amiably and worthily by the sovereigns that she was enchanted with her treatment, and publicly announced her regret for her haughty and ill-mannered conduct.

A few days after the Empress' birthday, the new

French Minister, M. Dano, who replaced M. Montholon—
recalled by Napoleon—disembarked in Vera Cruz. He presented his credentials to the Emperor in the palace, Grand
Marshal Almonte and the secretaries of the Grand Master
of Ceremonies having accompanied him in an elegant court
carriage. At the reception, which was very brilliant, the
generals and other officers who were in Puebla, the chamberlains, the equerries and the Palace Guard were present.

The feast of Corpus Cristi, on June 15, was celebrated
with greater magnificence than had up to that time been
the custom in Mexico, for persons who remembered the
days of the government of Santa Ana asserted that not
even then had there been seen so much brilliance and
splendor. The ball given by Their Majesties to the society
of Puebla took place on June 17 in the Alhóndiga.* Maximilian wore regulation evening dress, but the ribbon to
which his badge of the Golden Fleece was usually attached
was replaced by a collar of gold and precious stones.

A few days later another function took place at Puebla,
which was not only unusual, but beautiful and sumptuous.
This was the blessing of the flags of the Austrian corps, in
the church of San Francisco. The church, which is shaded
by old trees, is a marvel of ecclesiastical architecture, with
a double row of tall and imposing white pillars and a cloister as long and lovely as that of a medieval convent. On
the day of the ceremony the columns were covered with
garlands and festoons of foliage, while at their bases military trophies were arranged.

His Majesty was awaited at the door of the palace at
seven o'clock by Count von Thun, Colonel Kodolich and the
Austrian staff, all mounted. He was also escorted by his
own military staff and rode to the church with Von Thun

* The public granary which formerly was maintained in all
Mexican cities and towns of any size.

on his right and Kodolich on his left. I accompanied the
party in the capacity of chronicler. When Maximilian appeared, the Austrian troops were drawn up in front of the
church, and he was greeted by the stirring strains of military bands. A salute was fired by the infantry. His Majesty dismounted and, with his escort, took his place on the
throne, at the right of the altar. As it was a military ceremony no civilians or women were present in the audience.
The uniforms and their gold and silver embellishments and
the trophies of arms shone brilliantly in the light of hun-
dreds of candles which illuminated the wide naves of the
church. While the chaplain of the troops celebrated the
Holy Mass, Saverthal's military band played marches and
other military music. At the elevation of the Host the
troops presented arms, trumpets sounded, drums rolled
and another salute was fired by the soldiers in the atrium.

Mass terminated, the troop chaplain blessed a group of
new banners. As each company was named by Count von
Thun, the flag belonging to it was handed by Kodolich to
the Emperor, who in turn delivered it to the standard
bearer, who knelt before him and, pressing it to his breast,
took the oath of fidelity. At the conclusion of every oath,
the drums and trumpets sounded and the soldiers cheered.
As the Emperor retired the troops through whose ranks he
passed shouted vivas for "Kaiser Max."

By this time the Emperor had been absent from the
capital for two months, and preparations were made for his
returning there. Most of the high personages of the court
who had come to Puebla had left. The petitions for audiences increased every day, and more and more work was
thrown on me.

One day Maximilian said: "At present you will not return to your office. Write to Loysel that I have assigned
you entirely to my personal service. I will sign your ap-

pointment when we get to Mexico City. Also write to Don
Martín Castillo, the Minister of the Imperial Household,
and tell him that when we arrive Poliakovitz will be named
as his private secretary, and make out an order for me to
sign."

We started for the capital on June 23, at six o'clock.
The Empress, with Señora Pacheco, was in one carriage
and the Emperor and I in another. In the midst of a heavy
rain we crossed the Río Frío, breakfasted, and then went on
to the hacienda of Zoquiapan, where we spent the night. A
sumptuous apartment had been prepared for the Emperor and the Empress, but, as in Puebla, the Emperor
quietly ordered that his cot be arranged in another room.
Four leagues from Mexico City the Emperor joined the
Empress in her carriage, leaving me to escort Señora
Pacheco in the other. We were met at El Peñón [on the
outskirts of the capital] by many ladies and gentlemen,
mounted and in carriages. An address of welcome was made
by one of the aldermen, and amid the ringing of bells and
artillery salutes the sovereigns came to the palace.

1865

WE found ourselves established in the structure which for centuries had been inhabited by the viceroys, and which resembled an immense military barrack, rather than a government palace. Maximilian made radical changes in the interior. Then, as now, the right wing, lying to the north of the main entrance, was used for offices, principally by the treasury. But the left wing underwent great alterations during the Empire. Maximilian had all the small rooms in front [overlooking the Zocalo, or main plaza] thrown into one large apartment, which was called the Salon of the Ambassadors. It was suitable for the reception of foreign diplomats, balls and other elaborate court functions. The walls of the salon were tapestried with rich crimson silk, purchased in Europe, on which were embroidered the arms of the Empire and the motto: "Equity in justice." The tremendous and magnificent chandeliers had been brought from Venice. Also of European origin were the bronze candelabras on the staircase of honor, the white marble urns with the imperial monogram, and the statues which were [later] transferred to Chapultepec.

While inspecting the alterations one day the Emperor noticed that the beams in the ceiling were of cedar; he admired their richness which would have been noteworthy in any of the palaces of Europe, and ordered that the prosaic flat ceiling of white cloth which covered the precious wood be stripped off and that the beams be varnished and gilded. This is the state in which they still remain.

Likewise he discovered the fine carving on the columns

and arches of the principal patio and had it restored. The paving of the patio was renewed and the chapel, the state dining room and other rooms were rearranged. All the furniture was obtained in Europe, and was chosen by the Emperor himself, whose taste in everything was most exquisite and refined.

The palace china and crystal were from Sèvres and Bohemia. Each piece, even the smallest, and the linen bore the imperial monogram.[3]

A great part of the first floor of the palace was occupied by the apartments of Maximilian and Carlota. The Emperor has chosen as his bedchamber one of the rooms opening on an inner patio, for, as I have said, his retiring hour was eight o'clock and, since he slumbered very lightly, the noise of passing carriages and the conversation of passersby would have kept him from sleeping. The bedroom was between another room, where he received visitors, and my office, which also served as a reception room. The last was spacious, lined with filled bookshelves and provided with a large table which I used as a desk and several upholstered chairs and divans. In the corners were stands for decanters of water and red and white wines, trays of biscuits and sweets and fine tobaccos. These were replenished daily, and were for the entertainment of His Majesty's callers. Whenever Maximilian, who was a heavy smoker, came in without a cigar in his mouth, he took one from a tray. Frequently he would dip a biscuit in wine and eat it.

Accommodations in the palace were provided for Günner, the governor of the imperial residences; Kuhachevich, the treasurer, and his wife, who was first lady of the bedchamber; the family of Venisch, the major-domo; Grill, one of Maximilian's valets; and other attachés of the court. Because of the necessity of beginning work with the Emperor at four o'clock in the morning I also had a room at

the palace and one at Chapultepec. Offices for the members
of the civil and military cabinets were on the mezzanine
floor, on the south side of the palace.[4] The stables, coach-
houses, storage rooms and the like were on the ground
floor. The gorgeous state coach, ornamented with gold and
silk, which was used only on occasions of great solemnity,
is still preserved in the National Museum.[5]

I was entirely new to the court, and hence it became necessary for me to lose no time in identifying the different
functionaries and ascertaining where their apartments or
offices were, for the Emperor would frequently send me to
deliver verbal or written orders or notes to them.

I was already known to the Empress, for in Puebla she
had given me instructions. She spoke Spanish without the
least accent, very slowly, as though she were meditating
each of her phrases before uttering it. She was a trifle near-
sighted and almost always, when addressing a person, nar-
rowed her eyes as though to see better. She usually affected
dark colors; her gowns were high in the neck and adorned
only by a belt or fine white lace at the wrists and collar.
Her abundant black hair was simply dressed, and when
loosed fell to her waist, as I had occasion to observe one
day when the Emperor asked me to obtain from her some
diplomas of the Order of San Carlos, which had been
placed before her to sign. Carlota directed the maid to
bring me into her dressing room to get the diplomas, which
were on a table. She was seated before a mirror, in a long
white batiste dressing gown. A maid was brushing her hair.

Whenever I went into her presence I was announced by
an usher. I would bow and await her orders, and she always
said, "Take this to His Majesty," or "Tell the Emperor"
so and so.

Among the court dignitaries was General Juan N. Almonte, who figured so conspicuously during the interven-

GENERAL ALMONTE

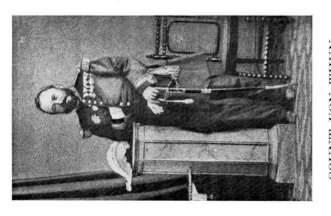

COUNT VON THUN

tion, the Regency [before Maximilian arrived], and the
Empire. Almonte was one of the most prominent personages of the Conservative party. Maximilian had much respect for him and made it a rule to seek his advice in difficult matters, which had already begun to arise frequently.
Almonte had been designated as Minister to France and
was leaving soon, since he was credited with being very influential with Napoleon III and was expected to be able
to settle the complications between the French and the
Mexican Empire, which were increasing every day.[6]

Next to Almonte in the Emperor's confidence was Don
Martín Castillo, Minister of the Imperial Household and
Intendant of the Civil List. He was the youngest of the
ministers, had been Finance Minister, and came from a distinguished Mexican family. The Grand Master of Ceremonies and Chancellor of the Imperial Orders [Don Francisco Mora] was also a man worthy of consideration.

Then came the Count von Bombelles, an intimate friend
and companion of the Emperor from their childhood, whose
personal affection for the Emperor led him to accompany
Maximilian from Europe. He was also held in highest confidence by the Empress. In his bearing the count displayed
his ancestry and breeding. He ranked as a colonel in the
army and as Governor of the Palace was commander of the
Palace Guard. Under him were Lieutenant Colonel Rudolf
Günner, Major Karl Shaffer and Captain Agustín Pradillo, all officers in the Guard.

Günner and Shaffer had been officers in the [Austrian]
navy and shipmates with Maximilian on his voyages aboard
the frigate *Novara*. Both were extremely jealous of any
Mexican whom Maximilian distinguished by his favors or
intimacy, Günner with hypocritical amiability and Shaffer
with open hostility. Pradillo was a spirited young man
who had been an officer of the *Zapadores* [sappers]. The

Emperor met him during his stay in Morelia, when Pradillo commanded his guard, and transferred him to the Palace Guard. There Pradillo immediately and deservedly won Maximilian's complete confidence as a loyal and brave man, for he was faithful to the Empire to the last and was always ready to yield his life for the Emperor.

The other officers attached to the person of the Emperor were Joaquín Rodríguez and Pedro Ontivéros, both of whom had been Republicans and had been taken prisoner when Forey captured Puebla. They were exiled to France and when it became known to them that Maximilian had accepted the throne, they presented themselves at Miramar and the Archduke made them aides. They were chosen to carry to Mexico Maximilian's message accepting the throne.

The most distinguished persons in Mexican society contested for the honor of holding positions at court. In support of their claims some advanced the nobility of their lineage and others their wealth and social standing. These were the considerations which largely influenced the selection as equerries of Don José de Jesús Cervantes and Don Joaquín Adalid. The chamberlains were Don Juan Suárez Peredo, Count del Valle; Marquis Felipe Neri del Barrio, Don Nicolás Campero, and many other lesser lights.

In like manner Her Majesty's ladies in waiting were chosen from among Mexican ladies distinguished for their beauty. Among them I recall Doña Manuela Gutiérrez Estrada, the Countess del Valle, and Doña Dolores Osio de Sánchez Navarro. The ladies of honor, who received an honorarium for their services, were Señoras Concepción Plowes and Pacheco and Señorita Josefa Varela. The last was of pure Indian extraction and a direct descendant of the [Aztec] poet-king Netzahualcoyotl.

In a country like Mexico, which since its independence

has been, and is, essentially republican, and where few possessed legitimate claim to noble titles, there were not many
who could prove their descent from the ancient nobility of
Spain. But, nevertheless, because of the lure of the splendor of Maximilian's court, everyone was eager to have a
position there, and a veritable fever of aristocracy and
nobility broke out, so that it was rare to find a Mexican
family which did not search out parchments, genealogi-
cal trees, or coats of arms to prove their descent from
counts, dukes, or marquises.

The fact that he was a scion of the house of Hapsburg
and of the oldest European nobility had not prevented
Maximilian from becoming a diligent reader of the en-
cyclopedists of the eighteenth century and being saturated
with the spirit of republican ideas. During the deluge of
petitions for court appointments, accompanied by allega-
tions that the petitioner was descended from such and such
a viscount or marquis dead these three or four hundred
years, Maximilian laughed and said to me:

"It is a great pity that we haven't a factory here for
turning out parchments and family trees, for we could
make a lot of money by it. These gentlemen seem to believe
that the blood of the nobility is blue, and forget that much
noble blood ran during the French Revolution and that it
was as red as that of the lowest plebeian.

"The beautiful motto of the French Republic," he continued, " 'Liberty, Equality, Fraternity,' is nothing more
than Utopian. To the real nobility of France—the émigrés—when they returned to their country, were added
adventurers, new-made nobles, the dukes, counts and marquises created by Bonaparte; almost all of them were as
plebeian as the humblest bourgeois."

While this craze to demonstrate noble descent was rag-
ing, the Countess del Valle became the mother of triplets.

When the news was communicated to the Emperor, he remarked that his Grand Chamberlain, the Count, was to be congratulated, not only for having three members added to his family, but also for having provided the Empire with three new subjects of proved, ancient, and legitimate nobility. [They were descendants of Hernán Cortés.]

Maximilian was generally thought to be very fickle, and it was said that the last person who talked to him on a subject influenced him greatly. In proof, the frequent changes he made in high governmental posts were cited. Only the friends who came with him from Europe and who held important positions had been kept in them. I frequently thought to myself: "If this happens to the big fellows, what can little ones, like myself, expect?"

With these examples before me, I fully expected that the same fate would befall me any day. But to the surprise of everyone, including myself, the Emperor continued to display every evidence of his confidence and loaded me with favors. He knew that I was fond of riding and one morning, when our work was over, I asked permission to use one of the horses in the imperial stables during my leisure. He assented without hesitation, gave the necessary orders, and from the following day on I shone on the bridle paths, mounted on a fine Arab. I usually preferred an English saddle, but occasionally changed to a Mexican. Shaffer, who was one of my ill-wishers, knew this. When we were in the smoking room one day after dinner, discussing the fondness of Mexicans for horsemanship, he said that it was bad for the horses to have the style of their saddles and bits changed, as we Mexicans did. As a result of Shaffer's insidious hint, the Emperor ordered that hereafter I should ride the Arab only with an English saddle, and that I take another horse when I wanted to appear in my charro suit. So from that time on I had two horses instead of one, which increased Shaffer's envy and ill will.

About this time the coming marriage of Marshal Bazaine and Señorita Josefa Peña y Azcárate was announced. It caused much comment, for the Marshal, although strong and vigorous, was more than sixty years of age [and the bride about twenty].[7] Doubtless the high position that Bazaine held, in Mexico and France as well, and the hope, later realized, of shining in the court of Napoleon III dazzled the young Mexican girl. Bazaine's happiness and glory lasted only a few years, for after the capitulation of Metz [during the Franco-Prussian War, 1870] sorrow, bitterness, and humiliation fell upon him. After his tragic death, she returned to Mexico, poor and obscure, and remained there until she died in an asylum in Tlalpan.

When the engagement was announced, the Emperor and the Empress offered to preside over the ceremony. They were married in the palace on July 26; the civil ceremony took place in one of the larger salons, and the religious rites in the chapel. At the wedding breakfast, at noon, the Emperor was seated next to the bride and the Empress to Bazaine. When dessert was served, the Emperor rose and toasted the pair, saying: "We drink to the health of our dear Marshal and Señora Bazaine. May God bless the union."

Then the Empress rose and embraced the bride.

The Emperor, who wanted to give the Marshal evidence of his esteem without wounding his susceptibilities, sent him the following note:

My dear Marshal Bazaine: Desiring to provide a proof of friendship, as well as of appreciation for the personal services which you have extended to our country, and taking advan-

tage of the occasion of your marriage, we present to Señora
Bazaine the Palace of Buenavista, including the gardens and
the furniture, on condition that when you return to Europe,
or if for any other reason you do not desire to retain possession of the palace for your wife, the nation will receive it, and
then the government shall be obligated to give her, as a *dot*,
the sum of one hundred thousand pesos.

The property was returned to the nation [when the Ba-
zaines left Mexico in 1867], but the unfortunate wife
never received a peso from the government and, as I said
before, died poor and neglected in an asylum.[8]

MAXIMILIAN soon afterwards elected to live at Chapultepec. He came to the palace daily, but ate and slept at Chapultepec. On account of its historical associations, he made
few changes in the castle. The rooms were papered and
painted, new furniture was brought from Europe, the
large drawing room on the main floor was changed into a
dining room, to the right of which was the Emperor's bedchamber and to the left the Empress'. The Emperor also
had constructed a spacious covered corridor, in which he
walked and I read his correspondence to him as he looked
at the marvelous view from the terrace. The gardens were
replanted and embellished with statuary and white marble
urns. The ramp from the base of the hill to the castle was
repaved and the stables were remodeled. The Emperor frequently remarked to me after silently gazing for minutes
at the glorious landscape: "Don't you think that this
should be called Miravalle [valley view], as my castle at
Trieste is called Miramar [sea view]?"

In His Majesty's bedroom was a button which rang an
electric bell in my room. As soon as he awoke, he roused me.
Washing and dressing as quickly as possible, I would go

to his room. After tapping lightly at the Emperor's door I would enter, with my portfolio of papers.

While we were going over them, as we did at Jalapa and Puebla, his valets would be dressing him in his riding clothes. We would finish a little before seven o'clock, when I would hasten to don my charro suit, lock my door and proceed to the patio, where grooms were ready with our saddled horses. Accompanied by an aide and grooms we would ride for two hours over the beautiful roads about the park and return to the castle. Occasionally when I felt more like sleeping than riding, I would suggest to the Emperor that it would be well for me to stay in my room and work; but, appreciating my intentions, and being keen to have everyone get up as early as he did, he would reply, half seriously, half humorously:

"No, sir; My Majesty will *not* permit you to stay here, for something might occur to me while we are riding that I should want you to note down."

At the conclusion of the ride I would go to my room, arrange such documents as I had there, and put on my morning clothes—light trousers, a black coat with tails or a frock coat, and a tall gray hat, as prescribed by court etiquette. The Emperor and I breakfasted alone and then drove to the palace, usually by the Veronica causeway, across the hacienda de la Teja, to the square of Carlos IV, or along the aqueduct.

It was on one of these drives to Mexico City that Maximilian conceived the idea, which he carried out, of purchasing land near Chapultepec and constructing a road that would directly connect the castle with the square of Carlos IV. This is the present Paseo de la Reforma, which during the Empire was called the Emperor's Highway.

Twice a week the Emperor granted general audiences immediately after reaching the palace. It was the duty of

a special attaché to prepare a list of those who desired to
see the Emperor and of their business and, confidentially,
what was known of their record. Generally the matters
were handled by the cabinet, unless they were applications
for charity. If these were granted, the names and addresses
of the recipients and the sum to be given each were supplied
me; the money was provided me by the treasurer, Von
Kuhachevich. I would ride or drive around and leave the
gifts. The sum was always at least fifty pesos and the
favored persons were very poor.

On audience days or when the Emperor, on arriving at
the palace, went into council, I was able to improve the opportunity to visit my family, but it was necessary for me
to be back by two o'clock, for a half hour later we started
for Chapultepec and dined at four.

It was the Empress' custom to be at the palace daily,
accompanied by one of her ladies, and hold her audiences,
but she always came at a different time from Maximilian.
Carlota controlled and directed her own expenditures,
which were usually concerned with charity and endowing
public institutions. The maternity hospital which she
founded is still in existence.

The Empress returned to Chapultepec in the afternoon
about the same hour that Maximilian did, in order to join
him at dinner. There were usually twenty at the table, including the aides, the ladies in waiting and the chamberlain
for the day, and me, with such other ladies and gentlemen
as had been invited the day before by notes despatched
them by the master of ceremonies. Agreeable topics were
discussed, all unconnected with politics. Their Majesties
spoke Spanish to everyone at the table, and if anyone
chanced to be there who did not understand that language,
one of them translated the principal points of the conversation.

MIRAMAR

CHAPULTEPEC

At the conclusion of the meal the Empress and the ladies retired to her apartments, while the Emperor would lead the gentlemen to the smoking room, where, standing, we smoked and chatted for half an hour. Occasionally after dinner, if I had nothing especial to do, and after all had left the dining room, I would slip away, through a small side door, to the stables, get a horse and gallop off to the city. But I always returned by eight o'clock to receive the Emperor's orders before he retired. The Emperor was aware of these escapades, but affected not to be and never asked me what I had been doing or where I had been.

Conversation at dinner one day having turned on the subject of superstitions held by various peoples, the Emperor described the *jettatori* of Italy and the amulets, charms, etc., employed to ward off the effects of the evil eye. He mentioned the bad luck attributed by the French and the Germans to the number thirteen and expressed his admiration that there was so little of this fatalism in Mexico, and remarked that strong minds should not be superstitious.

A day or two later the table was arranged for fourteen, one of the expected guests being an Italian abbé who was visiting Mexico. Court rules required meals to be begun promptly. Without waiting for the abbé, we seated ourselves. The Emperor, observing that there were thirteen about the board, summoned Venisch and whispered to him. Venisch approached me and said that, as there were thirteen diners, the Emperor requested me to retire. Scarcely had I begun to eat in my room, delighted at having escaped from the formality of the Emperor's table, when Venisch appeared with a summons to return. The abbé had put in an appearance and made the thirteenth diner.

Near the park was a large spring, which according to tradition had served as the bath of the beautiful Indian woman, Malinche, the favorite of Cortés. Maximilian frequently swam there at midday. A half hour before, his valets would take fresh clothing there, and four guards would station themselves to keep the public away. He would swim for fifteen or twenty minutes, pay five pesos for his bath, and return to the castle, delighted at having indulged in the sport which he so much enjoyed.

Occasionally he would drive about the park in a small carriage of wickerwork, drawn by two ponies, while I read letters and documents to him, and afterward rest for a few minutes in the refreshing shade of the beautiful old cypresses.

Twice monthly he would dictate to me long letters to the Mexican diplomats abroad, to go by the French and English steamships that sailed from Vera Cruz. In these letters he would describe minutely court balls, festivities, receptions, his journeys, etc. He would begin by referring to matters in the countries to which the recipients were accredited; then he would provide a résumé of what had occurred in Mexico in the past fortnight, always coloring his information to favor the imperial cause and discounting the reverses suffered by his troops. Finally, an extended account of the festivities. The clerks contended for the task of copying these letters, because when they finished they were provided with a fine supper and good cigars. I always addressed the envelopes myself.

Before retiring at night, the Emperor would turn over to me the late letters that had been received and if some of them were in cipher I would hurry to my room for the code and decipher them. If a letter was to be sent in cipher, Maximilian would dictate its contents to me, and I would put it in cipher. Sometimes as I was busy at this, he would smile and say jestingly, although there was serious meaning in his words: "Señor, if at any time any of these matters in cipher should be divulged, instead of the future to which you are looking forward, you would go to prison for the rest of your life."

"Your Majesty need not worry," I would reply, "for I am careful to forget everything in cipher, and a minute after I have read or written it I do not remember a single word."

April-September, 1865

THE Emperor's thirty-third birthday fell on July 6, 1865. It was the second which he had spent in Mexico. His father, the Emperor of Austria, Franz Charles Joseph, had on December 2, 1848, renounced his crown in favor of his eldest son, Franz Joseph. He was still living, as was Maximilian's mother, the Archduchess Sophia. The Austrian Emperor and the Archduchess sent their congratulations in long and affectionate letters.

Maximilian chose to pass the day quietly by himself, and remained at Chapultepec, leaving it to the Empress to go to the palace and receive felicitations in his stead. [There was an elaborate programme, including a *Te Deum* in the cathedral, a reception in the palace, both in the morning and in the evening, and fireworks and a serenade.] Meanwhile, from eight o'clock at night, the Emperor was peacefully sleeping, in the midst of profound silence and surrounded by sentinels and the cypresses of the Chapultepec wood.

A few days later, on July 10, the first of the sumptuous balls given by the court to the citizens of Mexico City took place. Invitations were eagerly sought, and as every family of wealth or of moderate social status wished to attend, it was necessary to limit the number of guests. Rarely had Mexican business seen so much money circulate or such activity among tailors, modistes, hairdressers, perfumers, etc.

The Emperor and the Empress appeared in the Iturbide salon at eight o'clock, where Bazaine, and the ministers, with their wives, awaited them, together with guests from abroad, who were presented by their ministers, according to the custom of the European courts. Each of the guests was then presented to Their Majesties by the Grand Master of Ceremonies in the ball room.

At one end was a throne, canopied with crimson velvet and surmounted by an imperial crown. Two palace guards stood like statues on either side of the throne, with glittering halberds. Other guards were stationed at intervals about the salon, each with halberd and helmet and in parade uniform.

The dancing began with the quadrille of honor, led by the Emperor and Señora Bazaine and the Empress and the Marshal. Across Maximilian's breast ran the wide, tricolored ribbon of the Order of the Mexican Eagle. The Empress' gown was of yellow silk and her costly jewels set off her beauty. The heavy brooch at her breast represented leaves of water plants, fashioned of emeralds, with dewdrops composed of diamonds. From shoulder to waist slanted the ribbon of the Order of San Carlos.

When the quadrille was finished, dancing became general, while the Empress chatted with Señora Bazaine and her ladies, and Maximilian passed from group to group. Supper was served at eleven. At the table of honor seats were occupied by Their Majesties, the foreign ministers, other members of the diplomatic corps and army officers of high rank. At one o'clock the Master of Ceremonies announced that Their Majesties would retire and the guests formed a lane through which they passed.

The procedure at all of the court balls was the same as at the first, save that at the following functions dancing continued until three o'clock, although the Emperor and the Empress left when Maximilian felt fatigued. Music was played alternately by an orchestra and the Austrian military band, conducted by the celebrated Viennese leader, Saverthal.

As it is the habit in Mexico to arrive late at the theater or balls, many of the guests that first evening came to the palace after the time stated on the cards and were refused admission. They were informed that no one was permitted to enter the salons subsequent to the appearance of the sovereigns. The lesson was effective, for thereafter all of the guests at the balls or other court entertainments exerted themselves to be punctual.

To Maximilian these balls were anathema, for they prevented his retiring at his usual hour and kept him out of bed. The morning after a ball, work did not begin until eight o'clock. He realized, as did Carlota, that meeting the Mexicans socially was politic and desirable. Hence it was arranged that the Empress should receive each Monday evening, without the Emperor. These receptions were known as *los lunes de la Emperatriz* [the Empress' Mondays]. Occasionally I was requisitioned to assist the Empress, and whenever this happened the Emperor was considerate enough not to insist on my joining him until six o'clock the following morning, instead of four.

Maximilian, on the mornings after a ball or some other affair at which he had been present, was prolific with comment. He was a close observer; little escaped his notice— the costumes of the ladies, the, to him, comical gravity of the elderly gentlemen who, he said, would have been more happy and comfortable in bed. Either at the breakfast table or in the smoking room, when surrounded only by his intimates, he would give rein to his sarcasm and jibes. His wit was pungent and cutting. Of a young and personable army officer who was married to a woman old enough to be his mother, he remarked that he did not see how anyone could have married that mummy whose fine clothes and jewels hid nothing but bones and parchment. One of the court officials and his wife were parents of a dozen children. Maximilian said that it was obvious that they made excellent use of their time and toiled so patriotically to increase the population of the Empire that he would take care never to permit the official to accompany him on any of his journeys, and thus compel him to lose precious hours which might be employed more agreeably and profitably.

Of certain ladies he said that he could see their ardor in their eyes and that they ought to be formidable women to love.

I told him a story of a chamberlain, who was blessed with an extraordinarily beautiful wife, whose charms the Emperor was never weary of admiring. Chancing to encounter him on one of his amorous adventures, I had asked: "How is it possible for you, who have one of the most beautiful wives in Mexico, to go on these adventures?"

"Answer me frankly, *amigo*," he replied. "Each day you have all sorts of fine food at the imperial table, but now and then don't you enjoy a meal of hot Mexican food, washed down with the white liquor of the country?"

While returning from Cuernavaca one day, in the same coach with the wife of the chamberlain and other persons, I sat next to the lovely lady. Weariness and heat made us all sleepy. As I drowsed off, quite unconsciously my head dropped on her shoulder, and we both slumbered peacefully until a jolt of the coach wakened us and we became the target of jests and innuendoes from our companions. When the Emperor heard of it he laughed and said that no one could have chosen a better place, and offered to wager that even if my eyes were shut I had never been more wide awake.

A certain count laid determined and successful siege to

the wife of a colonel about the court, to the knowledge of everyone excepting, as is usually the case, the lady's husband. The Emperor chanced to be looking up a date on the calendar, and said to me over his shoulder: "Don't forget to congratulate Colonel —— on September fifteenth; that's his saint's day." When he had left I looked at the calendar, and laughed to discover that the feast of St. Cornelius falls on that day. [A pun on the word "*cornudo*," that is—horned or a cuckold.]

About this time I was spending my spare hours at the house of an official, whose niece I later married. When I communicated my matrimonial intentions to the Emperor he said:

"What! You are scarcely twenty years old and you want to marry? It would be not your fault, but mine, if I gave you permission. Do you think I want you to be like a rabbit? By the time you are thirty you will have ten children and then farewell to work, to judgment, to rising at four in the morning. Wait eight or ten years and I will arrange a suitable match for you."

One of the incidents that enlivened the court that year was the arrival of the new Portuguese Minister, the Viscount de Sotomayor. His credentials were presented in great state on July 20. The Minister brought for Maximilian the Grand Cross of the United Military Orders and for Carlota the Grand Cross of the Noble Ladies of St. Isabel. In turn the Emperor conferred on the Minister and his secretary Crosses of Guadalupe, of different grades; and on the recommendation of His Majesty the Minister later gave Portuguese Orders of Christ to Minister Arroyo, Major Agustín Pradillo and me.

During the banquet which followed the reception of the Minister, the conversation turned on Mexican horsemanship, which led the Emperor to promise to give an exhibition of national sports for the diplomat. This was arranged on the plains near Chapultepec a few days later. Not only did a crowd of *charros* from near-by haciendas take part, but also Colonels Lamadrid and Feliciano Rodríguez. Stands were erected for the Emperor and the Empress and their guests. In his charro costume the Emperor left the castle at nine o'clock, mounted on his charger, Orispelo. Marvelous exhibitions of lasso-throwing were given by the *charros*. When they finished the *coleadero* began [throwing bulls by twisting their tails]. Inspired by the presence of Their Majesties, all of those who essayed this dangerous and thrilling sport outdid themselves, especially Lamadrid. After he had thrown several bulls from his horse, he dismounted and skillfully maneuvering on foot, threw a bull several times.

BEFORE going further into the details of court life, it is necessary to give the reader an idea of what had happened before I entered the Emperor's service.

The French troops entered Mexico City in June, 1863, after the second siege of Puebla, where the Liberal troops had fought so gallantly.

In spite of the French victories and the festivities arranged for them, Marshal Forey, a very keen observer, could not help realizing that the enthusiasm was forced. He was completely aware that the Mexican people as a whole would not tolerate intervention and that President Juárez evacuated cities by force of circumstance but continued to retain the affection of the people he abandoned.

On June 4, 1863, the Chasseurs of Vincennes occupied the roadhead of San Lázaro, on the seventh General Bazaine entered the capital, and on the eleventh Marshal Forey made his formal entry.

The French received from the reactionary, or Conservative, elements among the population of the capital—the property owners, the wealthy—an enthusiastic welcome. But the great mass of the people, the artisans, the workers, who as a rule are forced to bear the brunt of civil warfare, gave to the spectacle only their presence, inspired by curiosity, and preserved a sullen and almost hostile attitude.

For the first time the Mexicans in the city were required to lodge army officers in their homes. The billeting of the officers among the citizenry aroused resentment and ineffective opposition. But the dislike was speedily overcome, for with rare exceptions the French officers conducted themselves courteously and with consideration, and like all men of their race were gay, witty, gallant, and very attentive to the ladies.

For several weeks after their arrival there reigned great gayety, and wherever one went, in the theatres, on the drives, there were French officials in showy uniforms with beautiful Mexican señoritas leaning on their arms. To further placate the Mexicans, the camp of the African Chasseurs in the Alameda [the public park in the center of the city] was broken up, the place put in order, and morning concerts given that lasted from 10 A.M. to 1 P.M. These concerts became social functions and eventually many marriages resulted from the meeting of the officers and Mexican señoritas of good families, while numerous flirtations began in the Alameda.

Marshal Forey made a point of attending these concerts with his staff, in his full-dress uniform, gold-laced hat, blue trousers and jacket, and huge boots of japanned leather.[9] Forey was a big man, with stern features and a heavy mustache. At first his appearance tended to inspire fear, but on knowing him better one came to realize that beneath his rough exterior he was really a French gentleman of irreproachable and excellent manners. The Marshal was fond of children and gained the confidence of the youngsters who played about the Alameda. They would perch on his knees, playing with his sword and medals; he bought toys or sweets for them. As soon as he appeared the children would quit their play and run to him, shouting, "There comes Don Forey, our friend," or "There is Don Forey." But a few weeks after the concerts had been organized, the children looked for him in vain as Forey was recalled to France.

Then the Emperor came. For a period there was no cessation of social activities, but gradually the milieu of the court and of the capital began to assume a more serious complexion. There was discontent among the Conservatives [the original supporters of the Empire], for the Emperor himself, while realizing that there were excellent men among them, leaned toward the Liberals, as he regarded the party as progressive and with a political future. Thus it happened that little by little the men who had brought Maximilian to Mexico and to power were dropped or became estranged as they saw him surrounded by personalities who, because of their advanced political and anti-monarchical principles, could scarcely be other than his enemies. Being what he was—inherently more of an idealist and a dreamer than a politician—it was natural that he failed. He believed that it would be easy to end civil war and party division, by calling to his side Liberals who were willing to serve him. He thought that in this way an era of peace and national wellbeing could speedily be inaugurated, making it possible to do away with domestic strife.

Maximilian was confident that a hereditary monarchy was the most suitable form of government for Mexico. With this idea in mind, having himself no sons and knowing perfectly well that he never would have any, he formed the project of adopting the two grandsons of Emperor Iturbide. He summoned Doña Josefa, the only surviving daughter of Iturbide, conferred on her the title of Princess of Mexico, and committed to her charge Agustín, the five-year-old son of Don Angel de Iturbide, the son of the Emperor. Don Agustín, who had died several years before, had married an American. Maximilian paid her a large sum, and she formally relinquished her rights over her child. This accomplished, the little prince was proclaimed heir to the throne of Mexico.[10]

There was another grandson, Don Salvador, who at the time of which I write was sixteen or eighteen years old. He was sent to Europe to be educated, with an allowance suitable to his rank of prince. Don Salvador remained in Europe after the fall of the Empire and in Venice married into a wealthy Polish family.

Following the idea of Napoleon III, of creating in Mexico a Foreign Legion of sufficient size and strength to constitute a backbone for the army, Maximilian organized a Belgian Legion and sent instructions to Trieste for the recruiting of an Austrian Legion, the latter being destined to act as household troops. Nothing more effective could have been devised to sow jealous rivalry in the Mexican army. It wounded the pride of the Mexican generals, and the arrival of the foreign contingents increased the discord which already reigned in the army.

Meanwhile Maximilian was busy with matters of state from four o'clock in the morning on, thus stimulating the other public officials. He had already organized a Council of State, which was charged with the duty of drafting laws and governmental regulations and the preparing of those which were submitted by the Emperor. The Council usually followed his ideas, for it was composed of men from both the Conservative and the Liberal parties who were his personal supporters.

While this was going on in the capital, the French troops were fighting in all parts of the country. This clearly indicated that the Empire, far from being pacified, was in constant revolt. Nevertheless, despite the serious armed opposition to the Empire, Bazaine had followed the orders of Napoleon and sent back to France the first French contingents, commanded by General Laurencez. All the Mexicans who favored the Empire were profoundly disturbed over the departure of the French troops. One did not need to be a strategist or a great military expert to know that the Belgian troops were not in the same class with the veterans of Napoleon III.

This and other decisions made by Bazaine, who received his instructions directly from the French Minister of War, were wholly unknown to Maximilian [in advance]. Thus his mistrust was aroused and a certain tension marked the relations of the Emperor and Bazaine. Still, in public they appeared to be cordial, but several times in my presence, while I was writing in His Majesty's room, he and Carlota had long and important conferences over these matters. They spoke in French, but I could hear their bitter reproaches and complaints against Napoleon. They knew that they might rely on my silence and in my hearing were open in their criticisms and plans to save the Empire.

Matters about this time were complicated further by a serious defeat suffered by the Belgian Legion in the state of Michoacán. The Belgians were almost all boys, untried soldiers. Barring Colonel Van der Smissen and Major Tigdal, few of them were more than twenty-five. They had enlisted in Brussels, chiefly because of their enthusiasm to reap military triumph and glory in the country of Carlota, the daughter of their King. When the Belgians reached the capital they were reviewed in front of the palace by the Emperor and Empress. The Empress welcomed them and a dinner was served at which everyone was present from the colonel to the last lieutenant. Carlota was conspicuously affable in talking with each of them, questioning them as to their personal history, the part of Belgium from which they came, their families, etc.[11]

A few days after their arrival, the Belgians took the field in Michoacán, to reinforce the French Eighty-first Regiment, commanded by Colonel de Potier. On the advice of De Potier, Van der Smissen ordered Major Tigdal with three hundred men to advance to Tacámbaro, entrench there, and offer resistance to the passage of the Liberal general, Régules, who had three thousand troops [and who was on his way to Morelia, the state capital, to attack the imperial garrison].

At daybreak on April 11, 1865, the assaults were launched at every point. The Belgians left their trenches three times to repulse the attacks at the point of the bayonet, but at each sally their numbers were diminished, so that they were forced to barricade themselves in the church where they resisted until 10 A.M. By this time all the Belgian officers were either killed or wounded; among the dead being Captain Chazal, a son of the Belgian Minister of War; Major Tigdal, Captain Delaunay, and three lieutenants. The remaining captain and two lieutenants were wounded. It was not until the church was burning that the surviving Belgians, one hundred and ninety of them, surrendered.

General Arteaga [Liberal] that night reached Tacámbaro, and although he had taken no part in the battle, ordered that all of the youthful Belgian prisoners be summarily shot. Régules and General Riva Palacios opposed such a barbarous slaughter and overruled Arteaga. As soon as he heard of this rout, De Potier went after Régules, caught up with him on the twenty-third, and defeated him, sending him and his men scurrying to the south.

The feelings of Maximilian and Carlota when they heard of the defeat of the Belgians may be imagined. Carlota upbraided De Potier for sending out the little detachment of three hundred new soldiers, knowing that a greater force would attack them.

Eventually Van der Smissen was given command of all the imperial troops in Michoacán. Under him he had Colonel Clinchant with six hundred French Zouaves, and several thousand Mexican troops led by Colonel Ramón Méndez. Méndez was a brave Indian officer, nicknamed "Mejía the Second" [Mejía, also an Indian, was accounted the best officer in the imperial army].

Van der Smissen reoccupied Tacámbaro on June 29. To deceive the enemy, he pretended to withdraw again, taking with him his sick and his provisions. Arteaga fell into the trap. He threw his three thousand men into Tacámbaro. Van der Smissen struck by surprise. In an hour the city was his. Arteaga's cavalry fled, the infantry surrendered, and the Imperialists captured a flag, six pieces of artillery, and a great quantity of rifles.

This victory more than canceled the defeat of the Belgians, and the news was received with delight by the sovereigns, especially by the Empress. Carlota despatched a congratulatory letter to Van der Smissen, and the Emperor sent another to Bazaine. But they overlooked Colonel Méndez, who had taken a very active part in the battle. This served to create fresh discord in the army.

August fifteenth was the anniversary of the accession of Napoleon III, which was then a national holiday in France, and the members of the French expedition celebrated the day for the third time on Mexican soil. A *Te Deum* was chanted in the cathedral, Bazaine reviewed the troops, and in the afternoon Maximilian dined eighty of the French officers at Chapultepec. In the evening there were fireworks in the Zocalo. The festivities ended with a military ball at Buenavista, given by Marshal Bazaine.

THERE were two outstanding men among the leaders of the Conservative Party, Generals Miramón and Márquez. Miramón, who was a graduate of the Military Academy, had risen rapidly through all the military grades and, despite his relative youth, had become President of the Republic.[12] Márquez, who was born in 1820, began his military career at ten, as a cadet, and became General of Division in 1859.[13] Of unquestioned courage, both were expert and highly trained soldiers, and enthusiastic Imperialists. In justice to Márquez, it must be said that although his political adversaries reproached him for the executions of April 11, 1859, he had shown conclusively that he had done this by the imperative order of President Miramón.

Márquez was one of the first Mexican generals to place himself at the orders of Almonte [when he was Regent] at Vera Cruz, and afterwards fought with the French and entered Mexico City with Forey.

It disquieted some of Maximilian's advisers to see Miramón and Márquez so influential with the Emperor. They began to intrigue against them, seeking to convince Maximilian that the two generals were capable of betraying him, and trying in every way to induce him to send them out of the country.

Maximilian, who on occasions like this could always find a plausible excuse for getting rid of men who had fallen from his good graces, conceived the idea of sending Márquez as Minister to Constantinople, and thence to Jerusalem and all through Palestine. Miramón was designated to go to Berlin to study Prussian tactics, with a view to establishing German methods in the Mexican army.

These missions cost enormous sums of money, but this was considered to be unimportant, on the theory that, first, it was worth it to have possible traitors out of the country; and, second, that the presence of the pair in Europe, traveling and living on an ostentatious scale, would impress upon observers abroad that the Empire was stable.

There was a humorous paper published in the capital called *La Orquesta*. It marked the departure of Miramón and Márquez by publishing a cartoon which greatly annoyed Maximilian. Miramón was pictured as a student, setting out for school. Márquez was shown in the rôle of a pilgrim, bound for the Holy Land. Another cartoon which caused a public sensation and which was resented by Maximilian, represented the Emperor between two of his Ministers, Doblado, a Liberal, and Escudero y Echanove, a Conservative. The Conservative was offering the Emperor a packet of imported cigarettes, while Maximilian was helping himself to a cigar [*puro*, in Mexico] from a box held by the Liberal, and saying to the Conservative: "Thanks, señor; I'll try this horse." In the political argot of the period the Liberals called themselves *puros* [the pure, signifying that their political principles were purely pro-Mexican-Republican].

Maximilian was pacing the corridor at Chapultepec one afternoon while I read documents to him, when his attention was attracted by the sight of crowds running toward the valley railway. There had been a wreck and we could see the derailed locomotive and cars. The Emperor ordered that details be obtained, and they were brought him by his aide, Feliciano Rodríguez. There was a ball at the palace that night, but the Emperor asked the Empress to represent him until his arrival, late. Accompanied by Rodríguez we went to the Hospital de Jésus where we were received by the nuns, the physicians and the nurses and taken to the wards where the wounded were being treated. There were seven or eight victims of the accident, and three of them were in a very bad state. Some others—of a higher social level—had been taken to their homes. It was ten o'clock when we slipped into the palace, dressed and joined the reception. I changed my clothes in company with the Emperor in his room and one of his valets arranged my hair.

Sometimes when we were riding between the palace and Chapultepec, Maximilian would say to me:

"You probably hear a good deal of talk about me, and although knowing your position, persons in your presence always speak well of me, there may not lack gratuitous enemies of mine who, to annoy you, say unpleasant things about me. If they do, don't fail to tell me what you hear them say about my acts or myself, favorable or unfavorable, so that I can prevent the evils or abuses. I do not ask you to tell me the names of those who criticize my acts, or to take the part of a spy; I only want to know what they criticize in my government."

With this encouragement I frequently told him of the stories circulating about the capital, especially of the displeasure felt by many prominent Mexicans at seeing how he was almost completely dominated by the French, not only in military affairs, but in the administration of other branches of the government. There were in Mexico persons who were thoroughly competent to occupy important public posts, especially in the treasury, but foreign functionaries were put in office who cost the nation enormous sums.

For example, there was the case of Costa, a deputy in the French Chamber, who was succeeded successively by

Bonnefond and by Langlais.[14] Langlais was a minister without portfolio, but by Maximilian's orders always took part in the deliberations of the Council. He received the enormous salary of one hundred thousand francs a year, with fifty thousand for expenses, and at the end of three years a gratification of two hundred thousand. So the disgust caused the Mexicans by the arrival of this Minister-of-Everything may be understood.

Despite these difficulties, which increased daily,[15] the Emperor with his customary optimism saw everything in a more rosy light, and took fresh trips, leaving the Empress in charge of affairs during his absence. On August 24 we began a journey to Pachuca, and took canoes as far as Texcoco,* starting from San Lázaro at seven o'clock in the evening. There was a large canoe for the Emperor, richly carpeted, with divans and cushions. Supper was served at midnight by the indispensable Venisch. Besides champagne, it occurred to some one to bring pulque which, mixed with the champagne, naturally produced a deplorable effect upon the heads of some of the members of the party. This, together with the cold of the early morning, for the supper lasted until late, kept the Emperor from sleeping until five o'clock. We reached Texcoco at seven, where the Emperor received the usual cordial reception, which made it impossible to suppose that, outside of the sympathetic crowds surrounding him there, he was detested and regarded as a usurper and an adventurer in places where he was not known.

We drove in carriages to the hacienda of Chapingo, then owned by Antonio Morán, a chamberlain of the Emperor. We spent the night at San Juan Teotihuacan, in the best house in the town, where on the following day the

* Across the lake from Mexico City.

Emperor visited the famous pyramids of the Sun and the Moon. Señor Chimalpopoca deciphered the Aztec hieroglyphics on the pyramids.*

From here we went to Otumba, where we were received by Señor Carrasco, the patriarch of the place, whose family formed the bulk of the town's population. He had ten sons, all married and themselves fathers of numerous progeny. The Emperor conferred upon Carrasco the Order of Guadalupe and, in the name of the Empress, the Order of San Carlos upon his wife.

We remained that night at the hacienda de los Reyes, where we were joined by several persons from Mexico City, including the [Spanish] poet, Don José Zorilla, author of "Don Juan Tenorio," with whom His Majesty discussed literary topics. Dinner was served in the vast dining room of the house of the hacienda, and the host had a huge glass vessel filled with specially made pulque, for the Emperor to try. He drank the famous Mexican beverage and said that if one could obtain as good in the capital it would be served on the best tables. The day ended with a concert and a literary symposium. Zorilla recited some of his compositions, and the Emperor, who was an excellent poet himself, congratulated him and said that he had never heard Spanish so correctly spoken.

About noon the next day we reached the famous aqueduct of Zempoala. The Emperor marveled at this notable example of colonial architecture and remarking that the conduits were broken and useless, promised to have them repaired soon. Before Zorilla and his companions left us the Emperor appointed him reader to the court.

Upon his entry into Pachuca at six o'clock that evening,

* Blasio errs. The pyramids are pre-Aztec and the hieroglyphics have never been deciphered.

he was received by a delegation of notables of the city and managers and engineers from the mining companies, headed by Mr. Wald, who was in charge of the English company. Miners with torches escorted him to his lodgings in the company's headquarters.

ON the morning after our arrival at Pachuca, the Emperor caused me to be awakened at the usual hour—four o'clock —as though we had been at the palace or Chapultepec. Mr. Wald had asked what time he breakfasted, and at ten the meal was served with the same luxury as the dinner had been the night before. Before sitting down the Emperor said that he did not wish to discommode the company and asked to be permitted to use the wines and provisions which had been brought with the party from Mexico City. Mr. Wald demurred, expressed his appreciation of the honor bestowed upon the company by the Emperor in becoming its guest, and begged permission to act as his host during his stay in Pachuca. The Emperor assented, and later sent Mr. Wald a letter of thanks and a suitable gift.

After breakfast we visited the city and, in accordance with Maximilian's wont, the schools, the jail and the hospital. The latter was in charge of a young doctor, José María Bandera, an ardent Liberal, who the day before had refused to assist in receiving the Emperor. He did not expect that the Emperor would go to his hospital, but, despite his surprise, felt himself obliged to receive him courteously. Maximilian's affability won the physician in a few minutes. His Majesty expressed his regret at seeing the hospital in poor condition, and Bandera explained that money was lacking with which to improve it. Maximilian told him that fifteen hundred pesos would be furnished. Bandera asked to whom he should account for the disbursement of the contribution. The Emperor told him to no one but the physician himself, and invited him to dine with him that after-noon. Bandera accepted.

When we visited the Real del Monte mines, outside of Pachuca, there was a heavy fog. Maximilian rallied Wald, and said that the British were so much creatures of habit that wherever they went they not only introduced their architecture, but even the clouds and fogs of their own climate.

On our way back to Pachuca, the mount of one of the Austrian Hussars plunged into a deep ravine, at a danger-ous part of the highway. The man was killed. Maximilian was not told of the accident.

On the twenty-eighth we visited the picturesque haci-enda de la Regla, where the British in charge demonstrated the processes employed in treating ore. Near a beautiful cascade a typical English lunch was served, beef, potatoes with butter, tea, and beer. On the following day we went to other mines, including the Rosario, which was at the height of its prosperity. All of us, including the Emperor, donned miners' clothes, and tarred canvas caps, with candles at-tached to them. We rode on small cars on a narrow track into the shafts. Maximilian wanted to descend by a bucket attached to a windlass into some of the lower workings, but the officials persuaded him not to expose himself to the danger involved, although some of the party did, including myself.

Before he left on the thirtieth, the Emperor ordered one thousand pesos distributed among the miners who, in the evening, expressed their gratitude by collecting under the balconies of the house where we were lodged and cheering him.

We left Pachuca at six o'clock in the morning, accom-panied by a large party which followed us some way from the city, and we arrived at Tulancingo at four in the after-

noon. Maximilian was charmed with the place, which, surrounded by a rich farming country, was in contrast to
Pachuca with its mines. The customary banquet was
served, varied by the presentation to Maximilian by the
principal families of artistically woven baskets filled with
fruits and vegetables grown in the vicinity. While inspecting the hospital Maximilian talked with four soldiers, two
Austrian and two Mexican, who had been wounded and
left on the field for dead, after a skirmish with Liberal
guerrillas. He gave them the Military Medal and funds
with which to return to Mexico City and rejoin their corps.
The artisans of the towns were hosts at a dinner, which was
served in a park. His Majesty conversed with some of the
workmen who were presented by the archbishop and the
presidente municipal, and at dusk a number of ladies,
bearing candles, escorted him to his lodgings.

We left Tulancingo at 4 A.M. on September 2, reached
Texcoco at eleven o'clock that night, reëmbarked in the
canoes and were in the capital at five o'clock the following
morning.

THE COURT · IV

1865-1866

WE installed ourselves at Chapultepec a few days after the Pachuca trip and official life continued as before. Occasionally when the Emperor was unable to return from the palace for dinner, we would walk to Chapultepec in the afternoon, which provided him with opportunity for inspecting the new road and issuing orders concerning its construction. Now and then, if he got to the palace early, he would visit various offices to see if the employees were doing their work properly. No department was omitted, and he would stop in each room to inform himself of what every one of the clerks was engaged at, his salary, etc. If he found some of them chatting, smoking or reading the newspapers, he would speak privately with the head of the office, and suggest that he render a report on the work and conduct of the clerks individually, and remark that if they did not do their duty properly they should be replaced.

During a visit to the Academy of San Carlos (now the National School of Fine Arts), the Emperor praised the work of the Mexican artist, Reboull, the sculptor Noreña, and the architect Rodríguez; and expressed a desire to extend his patronage to them. He commissioned Reboull to paint portraits of him, one on horseback and the other standing, garbed as a Mexican general, with the imperial mantle over his shoulders; and Noreña to fashion bronze busts of himself and the Empress. He summoned Rodríguez to the palace and discussed with him at length various projects for embellishing the capital, one of the most ambitious ones being that for an independence monument in the main plaza. Rodríguez made a model for the monument, which is probably still in existence.* Maximilian also contemplated a reconstruction of the façade of the palace, after the style of the Tuileries and widening Plateros and San Francisco streets.

Complaints having reached him of the condition of the city prison, Maximilian inspected it one night, taking with him Feliciano Rodríguez, an aide, and me. He went through each gallery, cell, and dormitory, talked with a number of the prisoners and exhorted them, on their release, not to go back to crime but to lead hard-working, honest lives. He found everything in excellent order. Before leaving he inquired of the warden about the food and ordered that money be given to each prisoner.

Some nights later it occurred to him to visit the bakeries, as reports had come to his ears that the employees were treated like slaves. Rodríguez and I accompanied him. We rapped at the doors of several bakeries, but those inside, although informed that the Emperor was there and wanted to come in, responded roughly: "Emperor the devil! Go amuse yourselves somewhere else, or we'll call the police, and you and the Emperor will sleep in jail!" Finally we succeeded in getting into a bakery in San Fernando. The workmen said they had nothing to complain about, and he gave each of them a peso.

These nocturnal visits, if they were praised by some, were censured by the majority, who grumbled: "What kind of a ruler is this, who wants to find out everything for himself, instead of sending some subaltern to do it for him? Doesn't this prove how little confidence he has in his subordinates? Doesn't it make a fool of him, to be treated as he was at some of the bakeries?"

A tragic incident increased these complaints. A colonel

* The monument was never built.

named Carlos García Cano, who [had he been given a chance] would have served the Empire as quickly as the Liberals, was captured by the French. Among his papers was a document containing details of a plot to assassinate the Emperor and the Empress. He was court-martialed and sentenced to death. I had known him since before the arrival of the French. He was married to a beautiful young Mexican and had a small child. His wife, before and after the court-martial, sought out Maximilian at the palace and Chapultepec and wherever else she could find him, but he said that the matter must be decided by the court-martial, not by him. After the verdict she threw herself at his feet and begged him to revoke the sentence. But Maximilian was inflexible and directed that entrance thereafter should be denied her. The servants could not prevent her from forcing herself into the palace, even to my room. I tried to console her and give her some hope, and advised her of persons who might influence Maximilian and of the hour at which we left Chapultepec for the city, so that when our carriage passed she might throw into it a petition, signed by the persons whom I named.

Two days before her husband was to be shot, the unhappy woman stationed herself on the road near Chapultepec, and when the carriage approached threw herself on the ground, shrieking that she would stay there unless she obtained Cano's pardon. The footman descended from his seat and told the Emperor, through the carriage window, what was happening. His Majesty ordered the coachman to turn and take another road. Cano was executed and I never heard what became of his wife.

A few days later Councillor Félix Eloin returned from Europe and immediately reassumed charge of the civil cabinet and recovered his former influence with the Emperor. Loysel remained at the head of the military cabinet.

On September 16* for the first time the sovereigns celebrated the holiday in Mexico City. There was irony in the fact that although the people, in accordance with their custom, gathered at night in the plaza and enthusiastically cheered the independence of Mexico, the country was being governed by a foreign monarch! In the morning salvos of artillery, bells, bands, and fireworks announced to the Mexican people that they were celebrating their Independence Day under the government of an Austrian prince.

Their Majesties at nine o'clock drove in the state carriage to the cathedral and at the conclusion of the *Te Deum* proceeded to the palace and received all the high functionaries of the court, the diplomatic corps, the city officials, and other notables. The Emperor wore the uniform of a Mexican general, with the shining Grand Crosses of the Mexican Eagle and the Order of Guadalupe, and the Golden Fleece. The Empress was dressed in white and wore her richest jewels. Afterwards the Emperor mounted his horse and escorted by a cortège of generals and officers of high rank reviewed the troops of the garrison, who were paraded from the Alameda to Piedad. The troops then marched past the palace, before the Emperor, who stationed himself with his escort at the main entrance, and the Empress with her ladies, the chamberlains, and court dignitaries, who were in the balconies. The Mexican troops marched first, followed by the French, the Austrians, and the Belgians. As the Austrians passed, commanded by Colonel von Kodolich, the soldiers, who adored the Emperor, saluted with their sabres and cheered for "Kaiser Max." In the afternoon there was a grand banquet, at which were present Marshal Bazaine, the members of the

* The anniversary of the beginning of the independence movement in 1810.

diplomatic corps, the generals and principal army officers, and the ranking court officials. The celebration ended with fireworks and a serenade in the evening.

OCTOBER, 1865, was a fateful month for the Empire. On the third the famous decree was promulgated which provided the pretext for the council of war, in Querétaro two years later, to sentence the Emperor to death. It greatly impressed Maximilian that the sentence was pronounced on the thirteenth day of June, 1867.

Count de Kératry, in his account of the Empire, says that the draft of this decree was written by the Emperor, after meditating for some time, and that it was then submitted for the approval of his Council.* The count is mistaken, for the draft was written by one of the employees of the Ministry of War, on a large sheet of official paper, which was doubled in the middle. On the right was the original draft and on the left the changes, and on loose sheets some additions, made with a red pencil. The only writing of the Emperor which it bore consisted of the initial "M," which he was accustomed to inscribe with a half-flourish on the drafts of all documents submitted for his approval.

Kératry goes on to say that Bazaine had nothing to do with the promulgation of the decree, and that he did not know of it until after it was written. As a matter of fact, Bazaine was summoned to the palace on October 2. When the Emperor read the decree, Bazaine limited himself to asking that the death penalty be applied also to the *hacendados* [large landholders and farmers] who were in complicity with the Liberals. This provision comprised Article 10 of the unfortunate decree.

* The decree provided that all persons in arms against the Empire, who were captured, should be executed.

MARSHAL BAZAINE

JOSÉ LUIS BLASIO

This proves absolutely that the decree had been discussed by the Marshal and the Emperor and that when it was made known by Maximilian to Bazaine in its final form, the latter already knew the essence of it.[16]

During the last of September, 1865, the chief-of-staff of the [French] expeditionary corps sent a note to the Emperor's cabinet, informing it that Bazaine had received a telegram from General Brincourt [operating in the north] to the effect that President Juárez had abandoned the territory of Mexico, and had crossed the frontier at El Paso.

Naturally, the news delighted the Emperor, for Juárez' flight from Mexico appeared to end all resistance against the Empire and presented the probability that it would be recognized by all the powers, including the United States. In his ephemeral joy the Emperor issued the following statement to the nation, which began:

Mexicans: The cause sustained by Don Benito Juárez with so much valor and constancy has succumbed, not only to the national will, but before the law itself which this leader invoked in support of his claims. This cause, which has degenerated to that of a faction, is now left abandoned by the fact that its leader has quitted the territory of the country.

The statement went on to say that disorder was being continued only by some leaders, inspired by passion, and uncontrolled soldiers, and that from then on the government would be inflexible in punishing them if they persisted in their activities.

This was followed by the publication of the famous decree, sentencing to death all those taken with arms or who were convicted of belonging to any armed band. But notwithstanding, full and complete amnesty was proclaimed to those who should lay down their arms and surrender before November 15. This date was extended to December 1.

The Archduke-dreamer sincerely believed that the decree would serve as a bond of union between all Mexicans and end the civil warfare that had already cost so much blood. Everything tended to cause him to presume this, calculating, as he did, that with Juárez out of Mexico, no recourse would be left the other Liberal leaders but to yield to the Empire. Maximilian was ingenuously convinced that the decree would result in attracting Riva Palacios and many other leaders like him, who were the honor and glory of the Liberal cause; he also supposed that they would aid his government with their prestige and with their vast knowledge of the country and its people.

It was the Emperor's great illusion that if he could talk to Juárez[17] he could attract him to his cause, make him his ranking minister, and aided by him, and freed of the intervention of the French, he could govern the Empire wisely and inaugurate for Mexico, in its entirety, an era of peace, progress, and well-being.

But all these illusions of Maximilian were based on a false premise—he assumed that Juárez had quit Mexican territory. Hence the evil decree was issued throughout the country, and not only was the Emperor responsible for its consequences, but also all who signed it, who were: Don Fernando Ramírez, Foreign Minister; Don Luis Robles Pezuela, Minister of Public Works; Don José María Esteva, Minister of Interior; Don Juan de Dios Peza, Minister of War; Don Pedro Escudero, Minister of Justice; Don Manuel Siliceo, Minister of Public Instruction, and Don Francisco de P. César, Under Secretary of the Treasury.

As might have been expected, the decree did no more

than revive with greater fury the fratricidal strife that already had decimated the country.

The first important chiefs who fell victims to it were the Liberal generals, Arteaga and Salazar, who were captured on October 13 at Santa Ana Amatlán by the Imperialist Colonel, Ramón Méndez. The three hundred prisoners taken by Méndez were sent north and the generals were taken to Uruapan and shot in the same place where four months previously they had shot two imperial officials. These summary executions caused great excitement and were entirely irregular, inasmuch as in that locality nothing had been heard of the decree and it was applied without regard to the fact that the amnesty had not yet expired.

Maximilian, who, as I have said, was changeable and who rarely had fixed ideas, on hearing of the executions, ordered that thereafter, when there was question of the execution of any important chief, he be consulted before the prisoner was shot. He was too generous, for a similar sentiment was not demonstrated by Juárez when he promulgated his famous "Law of Death" on January 25, 1862.

Meanwhile the situation in the country became more and more complicated. Maximilian had planned a journey to Yucatán and had made all his preparations, to the extent of designating those who should accompany him, regulating their apparel, their places in carriages and on boats, etc. But the trip was postponed because of political and military complications.

General Riva Palacios at this time provided another proof of his chivalry, which was always recognized, even by his enemies. He had 187 Belgian prisoners, who had been captured at Tacámbaro, and realizing that terrible reprisals would follow when the decree of October 3 became generally known, he arranged for exchanging the prisoners over whom he had control. This saved the lives of altogether four hundred men, Belgians and Mexicans.[18]

After consulting with the Council of State and the ministers, Maximilian decided not to go to Yucatán, but that the Empress should make the journey in his place. She was escorted by Minister Ramírez, General Uraga, Eloin, the Count del Valle, the First Secretary of Ceremonies—Don Pedro Celestino Negrete, Günner, a chaplain, a physician, two ladies of honor, Señora Pacheco and Señorita Varela, and a veritable army of servants. She started on November 6, after her saint's day had been celebrated on the fourth with great pomp.

Two thousand Indians gathered in the main patio of the palace, and the Emperor and the Empress distributed silver medals; on one side was an image of the Virgin of. Guadalupe and on the other busts of the sovereigns.

Maximilian accompanied the Empress as far as Ayutla. Not wishing to travel on other than a Mexican craft, at Vera Cruz the Empress with a small number of her suite embarked on a miserable boat called the *Tabasco*, while the rest of her entourage voyaged on the fine Austrian corvette *Dandolo*. [The Empress remained in Yucatán two weeks. On her return she spent several days in Campeche and visited the ruins of Uxmal. She arrived at Vera Cruz on December 20 and was met at San Martín Texmelucan by the Emperor.]

During the journey and at meals the Empress spoke of the pleasure she was experiencing. She appeared to seek to cause the impression that she was untroubled, but [after her return] it was generally known that she and the Emperor discussed very seriously affairs of state, which unfortunately became more complicated daily.

MAXIMILIAN did not like the climate of Mexico City. He loved the tropics and [during the winter], when it was necessary to place stoves in his office and in mine, he decided to move the court to Cuernavaca.* The stoves were lighted in the morning and kept burning all day. They made the temperature as hot as that of a Russian bath. The Emperor reveled in the heat, but we Mexicans almost roasted. He used to joke with me about it. If he left the room for a few minutes I would throw open one of the windows to get a breath of fresh air, but on hearing his returning step I would hurry to close it again. Occasionally he would catch me at it and, between jest and earnest, say: "What are you thinking of? Don't you see that we're freezing?"

"No, sir," I would reply, "I see that we are frying."

"These children who have hot blood do not realize that an old man of thirty-two, like me, is as cold as ice. Close that window, and if you open it again I'll have a carpenter nail it shut."

I do not recall hearing Maximilian speak angrily to anyone. At times one might discern a regretful, reproachful or displeased expression on his face, but never violence or anger.

That winter, whenever we were in Mexico, Maximilian slept in the palace instead of the castle, for he felt the cold less in the city. But it was decided to go to Cuernavaca early in January.

Before describing our life in Cuernavaca I must mention an anecdote to illustrate the informal manner in which His Majesty treated those of us who were close to him. Before retiring he enjoyed a game of billiards with some of the aides, my brother, who was assisting me, and myself. The

* Sixty miles south of the capital, across the mountains, in the state of Morelos.

Emperor had dubbed me "The Child" and my brother "The Capuchin" because of his seriousness and taciturnity. One evening when we were playing he laid down a rule that the losers should be penalized by being obliged to crawl under the table. Most of those with whom he played were sufficiently the courtiers to seek to please him by losing to him, although he was aware that some of them were more expert than he. Maximilian did not like this and encouraged everyone to play as well as he could. On an occasion when he had lost a game by only a point or two he said: "I should pay the penalty, but I believe that 'The Capuchin' will be good enough to do it for me." My brother, accustomed to obey, scrambled under the table, which made the Emperor laugh heartily.

Usually on Saturdays he sought rest and distraction by picnicking in the country. Venisch would precede us with servants and a train of mules, laden with food, wine, etc. One day we went as far as the slopes of Ajusco.* Because of the rough ground it was difficult to transport tables, so the luncheon was served on the grass, where we were sheltered from the wind by rocks. We sat cross-legged on blankets and plaids. During these excursions Maximilian seemed to forget the dark clouds that were lowering over the Empire. Everything was free and easy, and at the end of the meals piquant stories and slightly off-color jokes were told. The Empress never participated in these picnics.

During one of them Colonel Lamadrid lauded the beauty of Cuernavaca and its climate so enthusiastically that the Emperor decided to go there.

We started on a beautiful morning, at six o'clock. I was

* A volcanic mountain to the west, overlooking the Valley of Mexico.

in the carriage with the Emperor, reading his letters and taking notes. We were escorted by the Austrian Hussars. At a point called El Guarda we breakfasted. During the meal those of us who were familiar with that part of the country told the Emperor of the wild region between Cuernavaca and Acapulco [on the Pacific coast]; of its natural riches, of the dangers which beset travelers and the discomforts they were obliged to undergo, even those with well-stocked purses; of the innumerable venomous reptiles in the forests, and of the disease called the *pinto*, common in that part of the country. Maximilian listened with great interest and projected a trip to Acapulco, observing that the more perils a region offered, the more attractive it was to a lover of nature.

A few kilometers before Cuernavaca a large committee received us and escorted us to the municipal palace which was to serve as Maximilian's residence during his stay in the city. As Maximilian wanted to come here frequently, he thought he could fix up some sort of residence in Cuernavaca. Señor Palacios, who was very well known in the city, said that nothing would serve as well as the so-called Garden of Borda, although it was so abandoned and dilapidated that many repairs would be necessary. The Emperor, when he visited it, was captivated by its beauty, its immense gardens, the spacious house and pools, all suitable for an imperial residence. In a few days the rooms were hung with tapestries, and the gardens cleared. Later, on his rides about Cuernavaca, the Emperor saw a site near Acapatzingo which he fancied and purchased a large area, where he had erected for the Empress a house after the Pompeian style, which was named *El Olvido* [Forgetfulness].

When we had been in Cuernavaca a short time, news

came of the death of the Empress' father, Leopold I of Belgium, at the Castle of Laeken, near Brussels, on December 10, 1865. Carlota remained in seclusion in her apartments for several days and Maximilian decided to return to Mexico City.

On January 15 Maximilian expressed his thanks for the condolences extended to the Empress in a heartfelt address, the notes of which I still have. They were dictated to me in French by the Empress. After eulogizing Leopold, he said:

"Strong in the support of my conscience and confident in the rectitude of my intentions, I contemplate the future tranquilly; Mexico has placed its honor in my hands and it well knows that in my hands its honor will be exposed to no danger!"

WHEN the repairs to the Borda estate were completed, in the middle of January, we returned to Cuernavaca to occupy the new imperial seat. Besides the usual suite, we were accompanied by Minister Pezuela and Professor Billimeck, a naturalist who had formerly been a monk, and who left the cloister to devote his life to collecting reptiles and insects for museums. Maximilian had employed him to gather a collection for his museum in an old abbey on the island of La Croma which he owned in the Adriatic.

While we were in Mexico City Colonel Feliciano Rodríguez, who had charge of the imperial stables, had busied himself with having constructed for the Emperor's journeys between the capital and Cuernavaca a new traveling carriage. It was provided with lockers for provisions and writing materials. The equipage was completed by twelve snow-white mules, all the same size, with blue harness. The coachman, the grooms, and the footmen wore charro uniforms of chamois, trimmed with silver, and wide gray hats.

Maximilian was delighted with the turnout, which excited the wonder and admiration of the Indians as the galloping mules swept past them.

The Borda house had been almost completely reconstructed. The imperial apartments opened upon the second, or inner, patio. The house had but one floor, which was approached by a flight of eight or ten steps. The first door upon the second *corredor** gave access to the Emperor's study. His bedroom adjoined, and next to that was the dining room. The corridor was provided with ornamental jars filled with a variety of flowering plants that flourish about Cuernavaca. Vines and orchids were arranged on the walls. Fishes swam in crystal globes and cages were hung containing birds with colored plumage.

Maximilian elected to work in an airy portion of the corridor, where a small table was placed for our use. There was a swimming pool, and beyond it spacious gardens, where the Emperor took long walks. The gardens also were a favorite resort for the Empress. She and her ladies ranged them with nets to capture butterflies with which to enrich Dr. Billimeck's collection.

Billimeck was an eccentric, very tall, rather fat, with gray hair and beard and thick, heavy spectacles. He seldom joined in a conversation unless it had to do with natural history, or his insects and reptiles, which he referred to as "little creatures of the good God." His knowledge of Spanish was limited, and when he could not think of a Spanish word he used its Latin equivalent. This made an amusing hash of his laconic remarks. He would start out early in the morning, his favorite hunting ground being one of the near-by sugar plantations that offered an abundant supply of specimens.

* Outside gallery connecting the rooms.

His equipment included an immense yellow umbrella, a cork helmet and a linen duster with capacious pockets. He rarely returned from his expeditions until nightfall. Often on our visits to the haciendas we would see him bobbing about like a gigantic mushroom, under his umbrella and helmet. He spent his evenings placing in alcohol the vipers and other snakes that represented part of the day's bag. Occasionally he would take off his helmet and display to us centipedes, scorpions, flies, grasshoppers and grubs pinned to the lining.

Maximilian, who was always more interested in arts and sciences than in affairs of state, would put in long hours with the professor, perfectly happy. I must confess that whenever the Emperor sent me to him with a message, it was always an ordeal for me to enter among his insects, and my nights were haunted with fear lest some of the poisonous creatures should escape from the boxes and cages in which he kept them and invade my quarters, which adjoined his.

A number of the young bloods of Cuernavaca formed themselves into a special guard of honor for the Emperor, called The Cocks' Club, the honorary presidency of which Maximilian was persuaded to accept at an audience which I arranged for at their request. The uniform consisted of black trousers, blue blouse, a gray felt hat with a black plume and, worn upon the breast of each member, a small golden cock. There was a captain, a drummer, a bugler and twenty members. They attended the Emperor whenever he appeared in public at Cuernavaca.

After spending twenty days in the town, we returned to Mexico City, where the presence of the Emperor was daily becoming more imperative. Money was scarce and the French government refused to supply more. Bazaine was known to have received peremptory orders to retire the

French troops, although the country, far from being pacified, was more rebellious than ever. Langlais, from whom so
much had been expected, had died, and been succeeded by
M. de Maintenant.

Almonte was in Paris on a special mission, as Minister.
Eloin and Loysel had also gone there to explain to Napoleon the true and difficult situation of Mexico. The cabinet had been changed almost completely. Ramírez had
ceased to be Foreign Minister, and the members had been
reduced to five: Escudero y Echanove, Minister of Justice,
Public Instruction and Religions; General Garcia, Minister of War; Salazar Ibarregui, Minister of Interior; Francisco Somera, Minister of Agriculture, and Martín Castillo, Minister of Finance and Marine.

One lamentable incident demonstrated the extent to
which the country was infested by bandits and that wherever the French did not police the country the citizens were
completely defenceless.

The new King of the Belgians [Leopold II, Carlota's
brother] despatched a commission to Mexico to inform the
Emperor and the Empress of his taking possession of the
throne. The commission was composed of General Foury;
his aide, Marschal; Baron de Huart, adjutant of the
Count of Flanders [another brother of the Empress]; and
two attachés. After disembarking at Vera Cruz on February 14, the party started for Mexico City. At Río Frío
it was assailed by bandits who killed De Huart and
wounded three of his companions.

Maximilian immediately obtained an escort and went
personally to Río Frío.* De Huart's body was brought to
Mexico City and interred with elaborate ceremonies. All
efforts at capturing the bandits or identifying them were

* About thirty-five miles from the capital.

fruitless. It may be imagined what impression was created by this affair in the European courts.

Worry over it aggravated Maximilian's ill health, which proceeded from liver trouble and intermittent fever, contracted on one of his trips to the tropics. Dr. Semeleder, his physician, was not skilled in the treatment of fevers peculiar to Mexico, and the Emperor was advised to consult a Mexican doctor. Dr. Rafael Lucio was at once thought of. He was the leading physician of the capital. The Emperor, reluctant to wound Dr. Semeleder's professional feelings, decided to summon Dr. Lucio secretly and commissioned me to interview him.

Dr. Lucio was a stalwart Liberal and uncompromisingly opposed to the imperial régime. He told me that there were plenty of other physicians who understood the treatment of fevers who would be glad to attend the Emperor, but that it would be very painful for him, personally, to do so. We discussed the matter at length without result. I went away without accomplishing anything. I did not report my failure to Maximilian, but merely said that I had not found the physician and would see him the next day.

At the second interview I insisted that the Emperor wanted no other doctor, begged him earnestly to accede, and gave him a slight outline of Maximilian's personality. Finally Dr. Lucio agreed to accompany me to the palace that evening at seven o'clock. I went after him in one of the court carriages, took him into the palace by a side entrance, and after presenting him to the Emperor left them together.

On the return to the doctor's house I asked him how he had been impressed by Maximilian. He replied that he had never met a person who was more distinguished or whose manners were more amiable; that the Emperor possessed the gift of winning those with whom he came in contact and that he had decided to treat him. His illness, he said, resulted principally from the constant nervous excitement caused in great part by the situation of the government. He would see the Emperor every other day. Maximilian informed me the next day that he was well satisfied with Dr. Lucio; that one could see after conversing with him for a few minutes that he was well qualified and not a charlatan, and that what had struck him most was the doctor's sparing use of words. He asked me what the doctor thought of him and I repeated the conversation of the night before in the carriage.

My mother fell ill of pneumonia, and the Emperor, who had met her some time before, permitted me to spend the nights at home and asked Dr. Lucio to attend her and to send his bill to him. Later, before we returned to Cuernavaca, the Emperor sent me to Dr. Lucio with a generous sum of money, which he declined to accept, saying that he was sufficiently paid by having incurred the gratitude of Maximilian. Dr. Lucio was known to be an amateur artist, and Maximilian liquidated his obligation by sending him a valuable painting.

On my birthday on March 19, the Emperor supplied a fresh proof of his regard and kindness by allowing me to spend the day with my family, after we had finished our routine work. The next morning when I went to my office Captain Pierron told me to "look on the table and see what the Emperor asked me to give you." In a small packet there were twenty-five golden napoleons.

WHEN the three months of mourning for Leopold I came to an end, the Emperor and the Empress went to Cuernavaca. The Austrian Hussars escorted them, with Count von Kevenhüller in command. He was a good-looking lad of twenty-five and since his recent arrival in Mexico had at-

tracted everyone by his elegance and distinction. He
quickly became the hero of numerous love affairs, several
duels and of other high-spirited adventures. As the eldest
son of one of the oldest families of the Hungarian nobility,
possessors of immense wealth, he lavished money with the
disdain of the European aristocrats of the eighteenth century. Later he became head of his house and a few years
ago revisited Mexico.

Among the other Hussar officers, I recall Barons von
Kulmer and von Malbourg, as gay youngsters as Von
Kuvenhüller; the three were inseparable companions, but
complied strictly with their military duties. Because of my
close connection with the Emperor I soon became intimate
with them and had part in their frolics; play and wine and
love temporarily made us forget the critical political situation of the Empire, although none of us believed that its
end was far off.

The court's frequent trips between the capital and
Cuernavaca had resulted in work which made the hitherto
almost impassable sixty-mile road safe and easy of transit
for all travelers. It was strongly protected by Colonel
Lamadrid's Municipal Guard, and cavalry patrolled the
wood of Huitzilac, which had been infested with bandits,
and made it as secure as the center of Mexico City.

As a rule Maximilian would spend two weeks in Cuernavaca and two weeks at Chapultepec, alternately. His frequent trips to Cuernavaca caused stories to circulate that
he had a mistress there, the seventeen-year-old daughter of
one of the government employees. Carlota's share in the
life there, where she passed whole weeks, provided material
for more gossip, to the effect that she was jealous or that
she was intent on ascertaining the truth of the stories about
Maximilian's love affairs which had reached her ears.

After the court had gone out of mourning, everyone

wore white at Cuernavaca except the Empress, who continued to dress in black gowns, save in extremely hot weather, when she would put on white, with black ribbons, which enhanced her beauty notably.

Carlota and her ladies were present at the dinners. There were frequent guests, the most regular being Von Kevenhüller. The principal target of Maximilian's jests during meals was Minister Castillo, who was a recent widower and personable. He was said to be courting the young woman with whom the Emperor was credited with being in love, and Maximilian insisted that she would be an excellent wife for the Minister. Castillo denied that he was interested in her and explained his frequent calls at her house on the ground that he was a friend of her father.

No reference to any of the stories about Maximilian was ever made at the table. Nevertheless it escaped no one's notice that he cast desirous eyes upon various beautiful women about the court, and when discreet mention was made of topics of gallantry the Empress would smile with a sadness that we all observed.

I was curious to know the truth of the rumors about Maximilian. During the day I was rarely separated from the Emperor and there was nothing suspicious which tended to confirm the stories. I was near him from early morning, when we began to work; then we rode, breakfasted and continued working; dined in the afternoon and rode again, and at eight o'clock I left him, after receiving his final orders. After that everything was profoundly quiet about the imperial residence. If the Empress was in Cuernavaca, she stayed up until ten o'clock, reading or sewing with some of her ladies, and the lights in her room could be seen up to that hour. In Mexico City there was no noise or movement after eight o'clock.

When I was in prison in Querétaro a year later, after

the siege, and the Emperor was dead and I was awaiting permission from General Escobedo [the Liberal commander-in-chief] to go to Mexico City, to obtain my passport and leave the country, I met His Majesty's valet, Antonio Grill, and José Tudos, the Hungarian cook. Both had witnessed Maximilian's execution and had wet their handkerchiefs in his blood, and were anxious to return immediately to Vienna and bear to his mother these pitiful relics. I suggested to them that we join the Liberal forces which preceded President Juárez' entrance to Querétaro, and passing for ranchers or provisioners, we would not be in danger from the bandits who infested the region. Finally, having obtained horses from persons who sympathized with our misfortunes, we left Querétaro for Mexico City, in the rear of the first Liberal battalion that marched to the capital.

On the way we talked of past events and especially of the personality of the Emperor. We frequently mentioned the estrangement that existed between the sovereigns, although outwardly their relations were entirely harmonious. I told Grill how I had so often noticed the separation of their beds. Grill, who had been in close contact with the sovereigns since their residence at Miramar, said that there they had seemed to be still enamoured and were always together, but that afterward, during a trip to Vienna, something had happened which alienated them from each other. From that time, although their mutual attitude before the world remained affectionate and loving, privately there was no such affection or confidence, and Grill himself had noticed their separation. As I had imagined from the beginning, some infidelity of the Emperor had become known to the Empress. This having wounded her pride as a sovereign and a beautiful woman, she had decided to adopt the attitude toward her husband which I had observed all the time they were in Mexico, naturally without seeking to

create a public scandal. It was very easy to believe that
what Grill said was true. But was it possible for a moment
to believe that the Emperor, in his prime, in full vigor,
with his high social and political position, his notable manly
attractiveness, his fine manners, his natural talent, his
dreamy temperament and his artist's soul, lived in complete
chastity during his stay in Mexico, where he fascinated by
his mere presence so many beautiful and distinguished
women?

"I never observed the least sign of amorous adventure,"
I said. "Did you, Grill?"

"You may have seen nothing," he replied, "but I saw
a good deal. The Emperor's bedroom was visited many
times by ladies of the court, who slipped in and out so
mysteriously that only I saw them, and frequently without
knowing who they were. How many of them, whom no one
would believe capable of it, yielded to His Majesty's desires!"

My natural curiosity led me to ask Grill the names of
some of them, but he refused to tell me and I never found
out who they were.

"Such things were easy enough in Mexico, at the
palace," I said, "for any of the ladies to whom you refer;
there were secret doors there, to let them in and out at
night. But at Chapultepec and Cuernavaca?"

"At Cuernavaca the guards were so stationed that they
might not have seen a woman going in or coming out,"
Grill explained. "Did you never observe in the garden wall
a narrow door, scarcely wide enough to let one person
through? It was always closed, but that door could tell you
many curious things about the persons who used it. I can
assure you, though, that a woman never entered the Emperor's rooms at Chapultepec."

Usually when in Cuernavaca we rode at seven o'clock to

some of the haciendas about the town, frequently accompanied by the Empress.

Early in May we returned to Mexico City; the Emperor's presence there was necessary because his relations with Bazaine were becoming increasingly strained, and furthermore the heat in Cuernavaca was uncomfortable. Although everyone believed that an open rupture was imminent, in appearance Maximilian's dealings with the marshal were cordial. Bazaine's first son had just been born. Their Majesties were godparents and the child was baptized in the imperial chapel.

As the Emperor wanted to give more time to important affairs of state whose solution was urgent, councils were held daily and the Empress was kept closely in touch with what was going on. She ordered me to come to her apartments nightly at eight o'clock and read my documents to her. She would listen attentively, as she paced the floor. Concerning some of them she would dictate her opinion; in connection with others she would give positive orders and place her initial or signature at the bottom. This would occupy us until ten or eleven o'clock. So it went on for twenty days. Then the Emperor took charge of everything. We were then at Chapultepec, for after our return from Cuernavaca Maximilian did not care to live in the palace. These nightly sessions with the Empress did not relieve me from joining the Emperor at four o'clock in the morning, to carry on the usual work with him.

As the tension relaxed a little, Maximilian decided to go back to Cuernavaca and there await the return of the Empress from a visit to the caves of Cacahuamilpa.* When she told of her trip with the grace and enthusiasm that were characteristic of her, Maximilian expressed his regret at

* In Guerrero, about sixty miles away.

not having accompanied her and promised to view the caves later; but unfortunately he never had the opportunity, as the political sky darkened day by day and the epoch of fiestas and journeys was soon succeeded by strife and tribulations.

PREPARATIONS for the evacuation of the French army were hastened, despite the urgent necessity for its presence in Mexico, where nothing had been definitely organized; and regardless of Maximilian's insistence that Napoleon had given his word that the French troops would remain for five years after the arrival of His Majesty in the country. And they were being withdrawn also in spite of the fact that on April 12, 1866, the French Minister of War had written that the troops would only be retired in three sections; the first at the end of October, 1866, the second in the spring of 1867, and the third in October of that year; making a total of thirty thousand men. It was now July, 1866, and the troops were beginning to be concentrated, as a preliminary to their quitting Mexico. The towns that the French abandoned were immediately occupied by the Liberals. For example, Guaymas and Mazatlan had been evacuated, and Tampico and Matamoros taken by the Liberals; and the Division of the North, commanded by General Tomás Mejía, had been completely destroyed.

Anxiously, almost with anguish, the result of the mission of General Almonte to Napoleon was awaited in Mexico. Almonte had taken the place in Paris of Don José María Hidalgo.* Maximilian complained that Hidalgo had not properly defended his interests. Almonte was depended on

* Hidalgo had been conspicuously influential in inducing Napoleon, and especially Eugénie, to commit themselves to the Mexican adventure.

to bring Napoleon to see the critical situation of the Empire and the necessity of permitting the French troops to remain; and to ask for the last instalment of money that Napoleon had promised and which was needed to relive the deplorable financial state of the government.

Bad news came from France. Almonte reported that he had had an audience with Napoleon early in May, and that the Emperor had listened to Maximilian's request for a revision of the Treaty of Miramar, for a delay of the withdrawal of the French troops and for more financial aid. There was never an instant's doubt as to what his response would be. His ministers, in council, unanimously rejected Maximilian's requests. Not only did Napoleon refuse to prolong the stay of the troops and to provide additional money, but he imposed new and heavy conditions for the payment of what had already been advanced, and announced that if they were not met the troops would be recalled immediately.

Napoleon's decision could not be kept secret for long, and general consternation seized upon the court and those who sympathized with the Empire. Maximilian, who was very impressionable, could not disguise his discouragement and dejection; his vacillations increased day by day. Among the high dignitaries some were of the opinion that the time had come to take a definite resolution, to proceed with energy and to demonstrate to the world that the Empire could live without the aid of France. Others, who were more sensible, judged that Maximilian should renounce the throne.

To cap these misfortunes, the government of the United States, where the Civil War had ended, began to assert its will. There was no doubt that the sudden retirement of the French was due to the Washington cabinet, which carried its audacity so far as to declare absolutely that it would not permit the intervention of any European power in the affairs of Mexico. This prevented the enlistment in Trieste of [more] volunteers for the Austrian Legion, which now included twenty-five hundred men, as the United States government notified Austria that it would withdraw its representative in Vienna if a single ship left European waters bearing Austrian troops to Mexico. Before this threat, Emperor Franz Joseph ordered that the volunteers be released.

The impression caused in Mexico by this last event was deplorable, as may be supposed, taking into account that information of it came a month after the announcement of the fatal result of Almonte's mission. To alleviate slightly the pessimistic effect produced among the public, a decree was issued providing for the creation of crack battalions, to be called the Mexican Chasseurs, but nothing could cheer the spirits of the Imperialists, who saw the end of their enterprise approaching.

During these days of discouragement the Empress provided a proof of her energy. She argued that questions of such importance should not be discussed in Mexico with Bazaine, or by plenipotentiaries in Paris, or much less by an exchange of notes. She decided that she would go to Paris in person to deal with Napoleon. The courageous woman never doubted of her success; she assured Maximilian that the force of her supplications would bring Napoleon to do what was necessary for the salvation of the imperial cause.

Inspired by the heroic resolution of his consort, Maximilian with his own hand wrote a long memorial to Napoleon and approved Carlota's plan. This happened a few days before July 6, the Emperor's birthday. He was indisposed and took no part in the ceremonies with which it was celebrated, designating the Empress to receive congratulations in his name. The Empress responded to the felicitations with these words:

"Gentlemen, I am happy to receive your good wishes, in the name of the prince who has consecrated his entire life to you and I assure you that his life and mine have no object other than your welfare."

The reception over, Her Majesty went to Chapultepec, so there was no gala banquet, no fireworks, no illuminations. There were other matters of vital importance to attend to; and no time to waste in demonstrations of a confidence or rejoicing that was felt neither by the sovereigns nor the subjects of the Empire.

In her little speech the Empress made no allusion to her journey, but she could not conceal her intention from those around her. When she returned to her apartment and laid aside her mantle and crown, her ladies begged permission to embrace her, in obedience to the affection they felt for her. Her Majesty was not unaware of the sentiment which dictated this demonstration and yielded to it. Sobs and tears accompanied the act. She regarded it as an unpardonable weakness to permit her emotion to be seen, and she retired. But as the episode could not be ignored, and would undoubtedly become public, the next day the *Diario Oficial* announced the journey in the following terms:

"Her Majesty the Empress will leave tomorrow to discuss the interests of Mexico and to arrange various international matters. This mission accepted by our sovereign, with true patriotism, is the best proof of abnegation which the Emperor could furnish his new country; especially as the Empress will risk yellow fever, which at present is claiming victims on the coast of Vera Cruz, and is so dangerous during the rainy season.

"This notice is given in order that the public may know the real object of Her Majesty's journey."

The Empress left Mexico City at four o'clock on the morning of July 9, 1866, accompanied by: Don Martín Castillo, Foreign Minister; the Count del Valle, Grand Chamberlain; Don Felipe N. del Barrio, Chamberlain; Doña Manuela Gutiérrez Estrada del Barrio, lady in waiting; Count von Bombelles; Von Kuhachevich, Treasurer of the Imperial Household; Señora von Kuhachevich, first lady of the bedchamber; Dr. Bouslaveck, ten personal servants and the servants of members of her party. She was escorted by a detachment of cavalry.

Maximilian, who was never to see her again, went with her as far as Ayutla, about twenty miles from the capital.

The Empress reached Puebla at nine o'clock that night, where a scene took place which astonished all who witnessed it. She suddenly arose at midnight, summoned her servants and made them take her to the residence of Señor Esteva, who had been prefect of Puebla, and was then occupying a post in Vera Cruz.

Carlota called out agitatedly until the servants in charge of the house admitted her. She walked through all the vacant rooms, and after pointing out a salon where several months before she had been present at a banquet, returned to her lodgings without explaining to those who accompanied her the reason for the strange visit. This was the first indication that her mind was disordered, although at the time no one suspected it.

The Empress resumed her journey at eleven o'clock on the tenth of July, slept that night at Orizaba and on the twelfth proceeded to Córdoba and Paso del Macho [the railhead]. There was a torrential rain; the roads were almost impassable. Her carriage was mired repeatedly and had to be lifted free by man power. Nervous and impatient, Carlota wanted to take to a horse, and was dissuaded only by the remonstrances of the leader of the escort. She imagined that she was being kept back, that the boat which was to take her to Europe would leave, although notice had been sent to the captain not to sail until the imperial traveler reached Vera Cruz. She reached Paso del Macho at one o'clock in the morning, rested a few hours and on the thirteenth at 2 P.M. was in Vera Cruz.

There an even stranger incident than the one at Puebla took place, and more publicly, in sight of the crowd collected on the wharf to witness her departure. When she saw that the launch which was to take her to the ship carried a French flag, she refused to board it and violently demanded of the port officers that a Mexican flag be substituted for it. General Tomás Marín, the port captain, sent for Commander Cloué of the French navy, and told him what had happened. Cloué, understanding that this was no time for useless discussion and not wishing to oppose the Empress, ordered a Mexican flag flown in place of the French emblem and conducted the Empress to the launch. Naval Lieutenant Leoncio Detroyat joined the Empress' party at Vera Cruz. Carlota thanked Cloué for his courtesy and said that she would be back in Mexico in three months. Her ship, the *Empress Eugénie*, sailed at six o'clock that evening, bearing that other unhappy Empress who was never to return to Mexican soil.

When she was declared insane in Europe, many and varying stories were current in Mexico, all absurd and unproved. One was that she had been poisoned by being given, secretly and by some unknown person, doses of *toloache*, a venomous herb, and that it was first administered to her in Puebla and later in Cuernavaca. Others said that she had been poisoned in Yucatán. None of these stories had any foundation. Wherever she went she attracted regard, especially in Mexico City, where even the most irreconcilable enemies of the Empire admired her

CARLOTA

AT SEVENTEEN, THE YEAR OF HER
MARRIAGE

CARLOTA

IN 1864

AFTER DECLARATION AS EMPRESS
AT MIRAMAR

CARLOTA

UPON HER ARRIVAL IN MEXICO

CARLOTA

AT TWENTY-SIX

magnanimous heart, and praised the maternity hospital she founded which did not cost the treasury a centavo and which still exists as an imperishable remembrance of her.

In the meanwhile Maximilian passed most of his time at Chapultepec, and for days did not go to the palace. The ministers went to the castle daily, and Captain Pierron also. The correspondence between the Emperor and Bazaine grew more animated, and served to intensify their differences. When Maximilian heard of Carlota's vagaries at Puebla and Vera Cruz he attached no importance to them, and set them down as feminine caprice. In his letters to Bazaine he continued to speak of the general pacification of the country—this when the Belgian Colonel, Van der Smissen, was retiring from Monterey with his forces, the French were abandoning Saltillo and the Austrian General, Von Thun, had been ordered to go from Puebla to Tulancingo and was unable to move his troops for lack of money.

Continuing his idea of winning the sympathy of the French, Maximilian had named General Osmont Minister of War and Friant as Finance Minister, to the displeasure of Bazaine, who protested that these duties were incompatible with the posts occupied by the two men in the French army. An indication of the manner in which the Emperor sought to compromise the French in the support of the Empire was revealed in the decree that announced the appointments of Osmont and Friant:

"These measures, which are in harmony with the mission of the Empress, demonstrate that the government marches in accord with its glorious allies and is exerting all the effort that the nation can demand to bring about the pacification of the country."

In a letter to Bazaine, sent a few days after the appearance of the decree, Maximilian announced to the marshal that, in accordance with the opinion of his ministry, he had declared a state of siege in the sections where there was greatest disorder, and added that the ministers thought that this should be applied to the entire Empire. By this it could be understood at once that Maximilian's intention was to compel the French, willingly or otherwise, to remain.

HERTZFELD, the first councillor of state in Vienna, and Galloti, the Mexican consul in Rome, who had been summoned by Maximilian, arrived a few weeks later. Hertzfeld was a naval officer and a friend of Maximilian, who had voyaged with him on the *Novara*, with Shaffer and Günner. His presence in that period of fears and uncertainty which had prevailed since the departure of the Empress provided consolation for the Emperor. Galloti was also an old friend of Maximilian, who had sent for him before to occupy a post in the government suitable to his talents. Galloti had always refused to come, giving various reasons but never the true one—which was his dread of the Mexican climate; he thought that yellow fever was endemic in all of Mexico. He finally decided to come, but made the trip with precautions: he did not disembark at Havana, and on arriving at Vera Cruz, where he was obliged to spend one night, he believed that he was dying and experienced all the symptoms of yellow fever.

After fifteen or twenty days Galloti decided to return to Rome, where his family was; remarking that he was ambitious for no more honors or dignities. He was very comfortable in Italy, he said, and had been led to come to Mexico only because of his affection for Maximilian. The Emperor let him have his way. He hurried through Vera Cruz and aboard an English boat. Not far from Havana he was stricken with fever and died.

Hertzfeld was close to Maximilian from the time he arrived, and had apartments in the palace and at Chapulte-pec. He spent long hours with Maximilian, discussing diffi-cult matters and the relations between the Emperor and the Marshal.

The amount of work I had had to do these last days had undermined my health, as I told Dr. Semeleder, and he in turn told Maximilian. It was then decided that I should be sent to Europe as a special courier carrying important papers for the Empress, and that when I had finished my mission I should have six months' leave for travel. I was to train two of the employees in the office to do my work while I was absent.

Finally, on August 7, I bade farewell to the Emperor and received from him my final instructions and the letters which I was to take with me. Included was a long cipher despatch which I was to deliver to Almonte when I reached Paris, and which he was to transmit to the Empress, wher-ever she might be. Maximilian said that after I had given my letters to the Empress, if she had nothing further for me to do, I might visit the European capitals at my pleas-ure; that I should not do as other travelers who contented themselves with visiting only Paris, when there were many other cities of Germany, Austria, Italy, and Switzerland that offered great attractions; and that when I returned I should have my old post. Günner, who in the absence of Bombelles, Shaffer, and Kuhachevich, was in charge of the imperial treasury, provided me with enough money for the journey and also with directions for obtaining more abroad.

Equipped with my credentials as a special courier, I left by coach at four o'clock on the morning of the eighth and was escorted by soldiers to Paso del Macho. Because of the rains and the poor condition of the road I did not reach there until four days later. I was in Vera Cruz on the morning of the thirteenth, at nine o'clock. I was received by Don José María Esteva, the Emperor's representative there, with whom I discussed at length the situation of the Empire and who told me of the incident connected with the Empress' objection to the French flag. On the pier I met an Austrian sailor, Sponza, who had been detailed by Günner to look after me and who accompanied me to Trieste. Four of the imperial servants, who had been dismissed and amply paid, were on the boat, homeward bound. At noon, on August 13, the *France*, as the boat which was to take us to Europe was called, weighed anchor, after taking on board 750 French soldiers who were returning home. During the voyage I was told by their officers that three ships would soon reach Vera Cruz to transport to France the remainder of the troops in Mexico.

On my landing at Saint-Nazaire on September 8, twenty-six days from Vera Cruz, I telegraphed to Almonte the cipher message which he was to send to the Empress. Almonte, when I saw him in the Mexican legation the next day, on my arrival in Paris, told me point by point what had occurred between Napoleon and Carlota,[19] and also that the Empress had gone to Turin and Milan and was then at Miramar. He added that she knew that I was in France, and that I should proceed at once to Miramar, to relieve her anxiety for news of Maximilian and of what was going on in Mexico.

It was Sunday, which prevented me from cashing a letter of credit, so I was forced to wait until Monday before starting by way of Vienna for Trieste, where I arrived on the morning of the fourteenth.

PART II

From Miramar to Rome

FROM MIRAMAR TO ROME

1866

I ALIGHTED from the train at the first station outside of Trieste, Grignano. Servants met me, who took charge of my luggage and conducted me through the beautiful iron gates at the entrance to the gardens of the castle, and to my rooms. I sent word to Señora von Kuhachevich, to whom I delivered the letters for the Empress.

Her Majesty received me a half hour later. She was in deep mourning. Her face already showed her intense sufferings; there was a slight melancholy smile on her lips. She received me standing and said very emphatically:

"Why are you so late? Since you arrived at Saint-Nazaire we have lived here in the greatest impatience; you should have understood how anxious we were and not delayed a moment in coming to find us."

"Señora, I stopped only two days in Paris and a night in Vienna, and I was tranquil with respect to my mission, for as soon as I reached Saint-Nazaire I obeyed His Majesty's, the Emperor's, instructions, and transmitted to the Minister in Paris the cipher message, which he must have sent to Your Majesty. As this was the most important part of my mission, I believed that I had complied with it faithfully. Nevertheless, excepting for two days and a half, I have spent all my time on railroads in order to get here immediately and place myself at Your Majesty's orders. By chance, I got to Paris on Sunday; the banks were closed and I had to wait over until the following day to cash the letter of credit I brought with me."

"Probably you are unaware that the cipher telegram

sent by Señor Almonte is full of mistakes and incomprehensible."

"No, Señora, I did not know that. But if that happened it was doubtless the fault of the telegraph company. It can easily be remedied, for I brought the original of the message with me, and can decipher it."

"Give it to me so that Señor von Kuhachevich can translate it immediately. Are you sure that no one has touched the Emperor's letters that you brought, on your crossing or on your way through France?"

"Señora, those letters have not been separated from me an instant, either on the boat, in hotels, or on trains. They have been constantly in a small portfolio, inside another which was locked, and the key was always in my pocket on the boat, and my baggage was not put in the hold, but was in my stateroom with me. Your Majesty can also see that the seals are intact and that according to the inventory not a single document given to me when I left Mexico City is missing. I also believe that Your Majesty cannot doubt my loyalty for a moment and my proved devotion to your person. This commission is another proof of the Emperor's confidence in me."

"I do not doubt you for a moment, but you come from America; you are ingenuous and suspect no one. That would not happen if you knew the intrigues of the European courts. I am always fearful of Napoleon, who is our mortal enemy."

Afterwards she said that she hoped I would be content with the hospitality of the castle, that the Emperor had written that he had given me a six months' vacation, and that later I might take advantage of it. She then ordered me to retire.

In the meanwhile Von Kuhachevich had deciphered the

code message and when the Empress had acquainted herself with its contents she quieted down a little. The message
had to do with what had happened in Paris with Napoleon
and what was to be done in Rome with the Pope, and
charged the Empress to bring about a favorable solution
of these matters. Von Kuhachevich told me what was in the
communication.

I recounted to him my first interview with the Empress
and expressed my astonishment at her supposition that the
letters which were securely sealed with wax had been
opened before she saw them. Both he and Dr. Bouslaveck
informed me that since her interview with Napoleon the
Empress had been suspicious of everyone, and that there
was no doubt that she was rapidly becoming insane. Upon
returning to Miramar she had adopted the custom of taking her meals alone in her apartments; occasionally she
invited Señora del Barrio to join her. She was attended by
Mathilde Doblinger, the young Viennese maid who had
accompanied her from Mexico. The remainder of her suite
ate in a beautiful dining room the windows of which overlooked the sea.

Dr. Bouslaveck presented me to Señor Radonetz, who
was in charge of the imperial residence, and to Señor Ste-
phaneck, the Mexican consul in Trieste. Don Martín Castillo was there, the Count del Valle and the Del Barrios,
and Don Gregorio Barandiarán, the Minister in Vienna,
with his beautiful Peruvian wife, who had arrived on the
night of September 15, on the invitation of the Empress,
to take part in the celebration of the Mexican national holiday on the sixteenth.

The night of the sixteenth at dinner Her Majesty appeared to me to be less sad; she smiled and her eyes were
unusually brilliant. Perhaps dazed by the day's festivities

and the manner in which she had been acclaimed, she believed that the Empire might still subsist without the aid of France.

When the dinner ended at seven o'clock, the Empress talked pleasantly for an hour with the guests in the great reception room, in which Maximilian had received the Mexican delegation who offered him with the ephemeral throne of Mexico the fate of Querétaro.

Señora von Kuhachevich informed me on the seventeenth that the Empress desired to speak to me. Her Majesty said that she thought of going to Rome and that she desired me to accompany her; that not only would I be useful during the journey, but that it would afford me an opportunity to see the city. I assured her that it would be a pleasure for me to do so.

It was decided to make the trip overland, by way of the Tyrol, as there was cholera in Trieste and the Empress did not desire to be quarantined in Ancona or Venice. That, at least, was her excuse for going by land, although it was the opinion of Von Kuhachevich and Dr. Bouslaveck that her plan was merely an indication of the new and extravagant ideas which possessed her and which daily indicated that her mind was rapidly approaching complete collapse.

The Empress ordered Von Kuhachevich and me to leave Miramar a day ahead of her, to prepare transportation [by coach] and accommodations along the route. We left on the afternoon of the seventeenth, and reached Malburg on the following day, by way of Villach, where the railway ended.

At Reggio we met General Leonardo Márquez and his secretary, who had come from Constantinople, and Don Alonso Peon de Regil, the Mexican Minister to Italy, who had come to meet the Empress. On the following morning we were surprised to receive a telegram, sent from Brixen, telling us to return at once, as the Empress had changed her mind and was going back to Miramar. When we returned as far as Mantua we found another telegram, notifying us to await orders there; the Empress had again altered her decision and would proceed to Rome.

At five o'clock that afternoon the Austrian troops in the garrison at Mantua were lined up from the north gate to the Hotel La Fenice, and a salvo of one hundred and one cannon announced to the inhabitants that the Empress of Mexico, Carlota Amalia, was arriving in the city. Her Majesty received the respects of the officers who commanded the garrison. Courtesy calls were paid her by the Austrian officials of the city, both military and civil. She reviewed the troops from the balcony of the hotel and heard their enthusiastic vivas. In the evening the city was illuminated in her honor.

We started for Rome on the morning of September 25 by rail. The Empress rode in the first carriage, with Señora del Barrio and Minister Castillo; Count del Valle, Del Barrio and Radonetz in the second; the Von Kuhachevichs, Dr. Bouslaveck and I in the third. There was another carriage for the servants and two cars for the luggage.

After crossing the Po (Kuhachevich and I for the third time) we reached Reggio, where a wealthy Italian count had prepared a banquet for his imperial guest. We arrived at Bologna at five o'clock in the afternoon, and Carlota was received with honors by Italian troops, who were paraded on either side of the streets from the railway station to the Hotel Britannica. We resumed the journey at daylight the next morning, along the Adriatic, to Ancona, where an elaborate breakfast was waiting and Her Majesty was greeted by the Mexican delegation to Rome, consisting of

Señor Velázquez de León, Bishop Ramírez and Señor Don Felipe Degollado. When we returned to the train De León was invited to join the Empress in her carriage. De León, who was a highly honorable and talented man, from the first had been affiliated with the imperial cause and had been a member of the commission that offered the throne to Maximilian at Miramar. Because of his ardent Catholicism he had been chosen by the Emperor as the man best qualified to deal with the Pope concerning the difficulties of the Church in Mexico.

At one of the stops a servant summoned me to the Empress' carriage. I found her talking earnestly, and with great agitation, with De León, whom she informed that I was the courier who had been sent from Mexico with Maximilian's letters, and the cipher message. De León knew me, for I had had a long talk with him in Ancona, and began to question me along the same lines that Carlota had during our first interview at Miramar: had I been careless with my luggage, had I been friendly with anyone who might be suspected of tampering with the letters, etc. I replied to him as I had to the Empress, that I was quite certain no one had touched the letters excepting myself.

I returned to my carriage at the next station, worried, naturally, at what I regarded as nothing less than lack of confidence in me on the part of the Empress. But when we reached Rome De León assured me that he had questioned me to satisfy Her Majesty and that he was certain that nothing had happened to the imperial correspondence; but that ever since her interview with Napoleon the Empress had been so nervous that she saw traps and pitfalls everywhere. Carlota had told him that although she did not doubt me, I was young, inexperienced and confiding, and that it would have been very easy for Napoleon's spies and agents to commit what she suspected them of doing.

Excusing herself on the plea that she was slightly indisposed, the Empress did not attend a dinner which had been arranged for her at Foligno that afternoon by the authorities, and dined in her carriage with Señora del Barrio.

It was dark and raining when we reached Rome at eleven o'clock that night, but nevertheless the railway station was elaborately illuminated and decorated and an immense crowd was waiting to see the Empress leave her train.

Carlota was received by a commission composed of cardinals, which had been sent by the Pope; by the diplomatic corps and many members of the Roman aristocracy. The [Papal] Noble Guard, the pontifical *gendarmes* and an escort of cuirassiers accompanied the party to the Albergo di Roma, in the Corso, facing the church of San Carlos.

THE entire first floor of the hotel was reserved for the Empress and her suite. She occupied the center salon, with balconies overlooking the Corso, and two adjoining bedrooms, with another room for her maid, Mathilde Doblinger. Castillo, the Count del Valle and the Del Barrios had apartments in the left wing and in the right wing the Von Kuhachevichs, Dr. Bouslaveck and I. Our dining room gave upon the courtyard, and the servants were quartered on the ground floor.

The Papal cuirassiers and the French troops who were still garrisoned in Rome alternated as a guard of honor for the Empress. During meals and at the change of guard the hotel was enlivened by band music. All day long the Corso was thronged with curious persons, intent upon catching a glimpse of the Empress, and while she remained in Rome the hotel was the center of attraction of the city. What most interested the Romans was the charro uniforms worn by the Empress' servants.

After breakfast [the morning following her arrival]

the Empress, accompanied by Señora del Barrio, rode out to visit the principal churches; and in the afternoon, at the conclusion of dinner, drove in the Pincio, the beautiful park on the summit of the hill of that name. As I wanted to know all the drives of Rome, I quickly procured a horse and, mounted on an English saddle, rode every afternoon. Once I passed the carriage of the Empress and as I saluted I noticed her smile and say something to Señora del Barrio. I was curious to know what it was and took the first opportunity to ask. Señora del Barrio told me smilingly that the Empress had said: "These Mexicans can't keep away from a horse. See how quickly Blasio has obtained one, so that he can show himself off. How happy is youth, to be able to enjoy everything!"

During the heat of the day Her Majesty remained in the hotel, and received visitors from one until three, including, on the day after we arrived, Cardinal Antonelli, who came to welcome her on behalf of the Pope. I took care to gratify my desire to observe the famous cardinal by being on watch when he arrived. He came in a luxurious carriage and when he alighted a lackey in gorgeous livery, knee breeches, a three-cornered hat and a powdered wig, bowed before him. The cardinal was tall, agreeable in aspect, with a lively and penetrating glance and a sonorous, insinuating voice. He was clad in a purple robe, with a mantle of the same color. The crowd in front of the hotel knelt, and he passed majestically, bestowing blessings upon the throng.

The cardinal talked with the Empress for about an hour. No one knew the subject of their conversation, for they were alone, and both kept it a secret, although undoubtedly they discussed the unfortunate situation of the Empire.

On following days the Empress was visited by almost all

of the foreign diplomats in Rome. Their presence attracted the idle Romans to the front of the hotel, to listen to the military music as well as to gaze at the diplomats who came to call in full-dress uniform.

Nothing in the way of service was required from me by Her Majesty, who granted me permission to absent myself from meals so that I might see the sights of the city, and told me that when she wanted me she would notify me the night before.

Official announcement was made to us that Pope Pius IX would receive the "Princess Carlota" and her suite at eleven o'clock on the morning of September 27. The cortège was composed of various carriages, in the first of which rode the Empress and Señora del Barrio, escorted by the Noble Guard. All of the carriages were sent from the Vatican. Carlota's was drawn by four horses, with lackeys in the pontifical gala livery.

At the Vatican, preceded by the Empress and the Grand Chamberlain, Count del Valle, we proceeded to where the high clergy awaited us. Some of the dignitaries of the palace wore black velvet—short breeches, jacket, short cape, and lace ruff of the epoch of Philip II. The Swiss Guard, in their brilliant uniforms, which were designed by Michaelangelo, were drawn up along the passage leading from the majestic stairway to the throne room. The uniform was composed of very wide trousers, falling to the knee, and a cloth jacket, both striped in brilliant hues, stockings similarly striped and low shoes. On their heads were silver helmets with white plumes, and each grasped in his right hand a halberd.

We mounted by the Royal Staircase to the galleries leading to the great salon which serves as a vestibule to the Sistine and the Pauline chapels. Finally we reached the throne room, a magnificent apartment, with walls encrusted with richest marbles and decorated with marvelous frescoes, representing the most glorious incidents in the lives of the popes. At the end of the salon was a great throne, draped with red velvet bearing the arms of the Papal States. In a red and gold chair was seated the high Pontiff of the Catholic Church. He was arrayed in a cassock of fine white wool and a mantle of the same material and color covered his shoulders. Two of the Swiss guarded the throne on either side and about it were clustered many cardinals, bishops and other ecclesiastical dignitaries.

As Carlota approached the throne the Pope arose. She knelt to kiss his sandal, but he stopped her and extending his right hand permitted her only to press her lips to the papal ring. He invited her to take a seat at his right. All who accompanied her filed before His Holiness, knelt and kissed his sandal. He then blessed us and everyone retired, leaving the Pope and Carlota alone.

I have never forgotten the impression created by the majestic old man who at that time was head of the Church. Pius IX was then seventy-four years of age, tall, somewhat stout, of affable expression, with lively eyes and a soft and harmonious voice.

While awaiting the conclusion of the audience we were told by the attendants that we might visit the art galleries and some of the salons of the palace, which we did, including the Sistine and Pauline chapels, the courtyard of St. Damaso and the rooms of Raphael. We were about to inspect the Vatican gardens, when we were notified that the audience was ended and that the Empress was waiting for us, in order to depart. She was escorted to her carriage by the cardinals and other prelates. We all waited silently and anxiously to know the result of the audience.

On our arrival at the hotel we accompanied the Empress to her salon, and waited eagerly to have her tell us something that would quell our anxiety. But gloomy and taciturn, she merely bowed and said briefly: "You may retire." She ordered food served to her alone in her apartments and shut herself up without permitting anyone to speak to her.

As may be supposed, the greatest consternation prevailed among us. That afternoon the Empress summoned the Count del Valle and told him to arrange with the military authorities to withdraw the guard and the bands. She said she wanted no music, or honors of any kind paid her. She also had an interview with De León, to whom she communicated in detail the result of her audience with the Pope. The Pope, two days later, on September 29, returned her visit. He was accompanied by his prelates and guard. Carlota received him in her salon and conversed with him for a long time. When they finished we were summoned to receive the Pope's blessing.

Carlota continued to seclude herself, without desiring to talk to anyone. On the afternoon of the thirtieth she ordered her carriage and directed Señora del Barrio to accompany her. It was about six o'clock. Señora del Barrio was surprised to hear the Empress say that she wished to be driven to the Vatican.

She wore deep mourning, a cloak of black velvet, and a small bonnet with black silk ribbons tied under her chin. As she descended the staircase, we could see that her face was haggard, her eyes sunken, and her cheeks blazing—symptoms of the intense fever that had consumed her in recent days.

At the entrance to the Vatican she dismissed the coachman and told him to return to the hotel and not to come back for her. She ascended the staircase and asked to see the Pope. He received her immediately. Carlota demanded shelter. She said that the Vatican was the only place where she could be safe from the assassins who had been sent by Napoleon to kill her, and from her faithless ministers and servants who were in collusion with him.

Kneeling before the Pope and sobbing, almost shrieking, she implored him to protect her, saying that she would not rise until she had obtained the asylum which she asked. The Pope sought to calm her by speaking to her kindly and gently. He told her that she was mistaken, that no one wanted to assassinate her, and that all of us Mexicans who were with her were faithful and devoted. But he was unable to subdue her terrible nervous excitement. She repeated that no one could compel her to leave the Vatican and that if accommodations were not provided for her she would spend the night in the corridors.

The struggle went on and the night advanced. The Pope consulted with some of those about him as to what course to adopt, and sent for Señores del Valle, Castillo, and del Barrio, who hastened to answer his summons. They were apprised of the situation by the Pontiff's secretary, and called the Empress' physician. He stated that she was suffering from a grave attack of mental aberration, that probably she would lose her mind permanently, and indicated that the only way of calming her a trifle would be to permit her to remain for the time being in the Vatican as she desired and keep her from seeing any of the persons of whom she was suspicious.

In accordance with the physician's advice an apartment was prepared for her, where the Empress was to spend the night, in company with Señora del Barrio and Mathilde Doblinger. The rest of us considered what to do next. The Pope's concern, and his consent to Carlota's spending the night in the Vatican, were communicated to us by his secretary. Late at night we all returned to the hotel, profoundly affected by what had happened, as may well be understood,

SEÑORA DEL BARRIO

SEÑORA DE
SÁNCHEZ NAVARRO

and reluctant to credit the fact. The next day the report circulated through Rome that the unfortunate Empress had become insane.

To the end of adopting practical measures for dealing with the situation, a conference was held by Castillo, Del Valle, Del Barrio, Degollado, and Bishop Ramírez. They decided to wait and see what might develop the next day, October first. That day a messenger came from the Pope, saying that Carlota was calmer and had been convinced that she ought to return to the hotel. She had been told that all of the persons whom she suspected had left Rome; for this reason it was advisable that none of her suite allow themselves to be seen by her. The Pope also asked what had been decided upon, and suggested that someone be sent immediately to Mexico to inform the Emperor and to provide him with the details of the phases of the Empress' malady.

Naturally, no one cared to assume this delicate and unhappy mission. Finally Dr. Bouslaveck was chosen. It was also agreed to notify the Empress' brother, King Leopold, so that he might act while Maximilian was deciding where Carlota should be taken. While these matters were being discussed word came that Carlota was on her way back to the hotel. We all hid ourselves, but in places from which we could see the Empress alight from the closed carriage in which she had ridden. Accompanied by Señora del Barrio and the faithful Mathilde, she walked up the stairs and, dismissing the lady of honor, she locked herself in her apartments with the maid. Señora del Barrio told us of the night in the Vatican. The Empress had walked the floor incessantly, talking incoherently and refusing to eat or sleep. At daybreak, the physician and the Pope's secretary succeeded in quieting her and induced her to return to the hotel.

In a few minutes the Empress sent Doblinger to summon Señora von Kuhachevich. She said to her:

"I never would have believed that a person like you, whom I have known for so many years and loaded with favors and to whom I have given my love and confidence, would sell herself to Napoleon's agents so that they might poison me."

The poor woman threw herself at Carlota's feet, sobbing and protesting, but the Empress refused to listen and violently ordered:

"Leave at once, Señora, and say to your accomplices that I have discovered their plots and that I know who the traitors are. Tell the Count del Valle, your husband and Dr. Bouslaveck to flee, if they do not want to be arrested at once. You, too; I never want to hear your name."

Señora von Kuhachevich came away weeping and fully convinced that the Empress had completely lost her reason. Carlota then summoned Señora del Barrio, got into a carriage and ordered the coachman to drive to a fountain. He stopped at the first one they came to. Carlota got out, with a glass pitcher in her hand, and filled it with water. She then returned to the hotel and proceeded to her apartments, by way of corridors and courtyards that were entirely deserted, as all her followers had been given orders to keep out of sight so as not to aggravate her illness by their presence.

Mathilde in the meantime had procured a small iron stove, charcoal, two live chickens and a basket of eggs. The food was to be cooked in Her Majesty's presence, for she insisted upon eating nothing which she had not seen prepared and drinking no water that she herself had not obtained from the city fountains. The maid sought to persuade her to eat fruit, bread, etc., but Carlota refused, saying that everything was poisoned. Mathilde was compelled to kill, dress, and cook the chickens in the Empress' apartments.

Carlota would not disrobe at night or go to bed, but paced back and forth in her bedroom. At dawn she would rest for a short time in an armchair. At the end of a few days Mathilde was worn out and was almost insane herself. She was obliged to exercise a great deal of guile to accustom the Empress to the sight of another maid, a Roman, of whom Carlota was not suspicious and whom Mathilde induced to assist her.

A decision was made to cable Maximilian, through Von Hertzfeld, the truth concerning the Empress' state. The cable read:

"Her Majesty, the Empress Carlota, on October 4 was attacked by a very serious cerebral congestion. The august princess has been conducted to Miramar."

It was also decided that Dr. Bouslaveck should go to Mexico by way of New York, which was the quickest way he could get there, to explain to Maximilian in detail the development of the Empress' illness and the probabilities of her cure. Leopold II was telegraphed to, and replied that Carlota's other brother, the Count of Flanders, had left Brussels to take her to Miramar and to consult there with specialists on her treatment; and that the Count would reach Rome on October 7.

On the morning of the seventh the Empress asked Señora del Barrio if I was in Rome. When the lady of honor answered in the affirmative, I was conducted to her apartments. I found her standing, erect as always, dressed in mourning, in a high-necked gown, with her hair carefully dressed, for her insanity had not caused her to be careless of her appearance. She spoke pleasantly, but sadly:

"You have seen much in Rome and want to go to other European cities, and you may; but first, I want you to write some decrees for me to sign. Sit down and do it."

On a small table I began to write, from Her Majesty's dictation:

"Carlota, Empress of Mexico:

"Inasmuch as our Grand Chamberlain, Señor Juan Suárez Peredo, Count del Valle de Orizaba, has taken part in a conspiracy to attempt the life of his sovereign, we have thought well to deprive him, as we do by this, of all of his titles, charges and honors, and to command him to leave the court without returning to it for any reason; and to communicate to His Majesty, the Emperor Maximilian, this disposition which I have signed and which is for the information of our officer in charge of the Civil List and Minister of the Imperial Household.

"Rome, October 7, 1866."

I read the document to her. She was satisfied with it and said:

"Write others for the dismissal of Señor Felipe Neri del Barrio, Marquis del Apartado, from the office of chamberlain; Dr. Bouslaveck from the post of physician of the bedchamber; Señor von Kuhachevich as Treasurer of the Imperial Household; Señora von Kuhachevich as first lady of the bedchamber, and Señor Martín Castillo, officer of the Civil List and Minister of the Imperial Household."

My readers can readily understand that at the moment the only thing to do was to obey and not to oppose in the least the princess' orders, so as not to aggravate her insanity. For a minute, nevertheless, I thought of asking how it would be possible for Señor Castillo to obey the decrees if he himself were dismissed, or how he could sign them if, as she had been led to believe, he had already left Rome. Everything seemed peaceful in the room, and occasionally I would steal a glance at the Empress' face, upon which a few days of emotion and suffering had wrought so many changes. It was haggard, the cheeks sunken and flushed; her eyes had a wild expression and, when her attention was not fixed, roamed vaguely and uncertainly as though in search of absent figures or far-away scenes.

I could also observe the fittings of the room, including a large wooden bed with a silken canopy, which showed no signs of having been occupied for nights. On the night table by the bed was a candlestick, with a half-consumed taper and a small gold watch. There was an armchair at the foot of the bed, in which the Empress took her brief intervals of rest; a wardrobe with mirrors, a dressing table with silver toilet articles and a silver pitcher, some chairs upholstered in brocade, and a table, on which was the charcoal stove used by Mathilde in cooking the Empress' meals. Some hens were tied to the legs of the table, and on it were eggs and the pitcher of water which Carlota procured for herself. During our last days in Rome I saw her stop her carriage at the beautiful fountain of Trevi, fill her crystal pitcher from one of its splendid jets, and reënter the carriage without paying attention to anything, without recognizing me or anyone.

When I had written the decrees I stood up to ask for and receive orders. She said that inasmuch as I had permission to remain in Europe for six months and as she had kept me for some time, I might leave Rome whenever I liked. She thanked me for having accompanied her to Rome, and before dismissing me asked me to seek for Señor Castillo, so that he might present himself to sign the decrees that I had written and take note of them. I remarked that he was not in the hotel and that probably he had left Rome. But the Empress with some emphasis said:

"Never mind. Look for him until you find him and have him come as soon as possible."

I asked permission to kiss her hand, which I did, kneeling and with tears in my eyes.

Castillo and the others were waiting anxiously for me when I emerged from the Empress' apartments. I told them all that had happened, including my commission to hunt for Castillo, so that he might sign the decrees, which I had left on the table in Carlota's room. The opinion was expressed by some that Castillo should present himself and sign the decrees, take them and destroy them. But he said, and with reason, that if he signed such absurd documents it might well happen that the Empress would not give them to him, but send them directly to the Emperor. Finally it was decided to tell the Empress that Castillo had left Rome, but that he had been sent for. In the meanwhile, the Count of Flanders would arrive and then it could be seen what was best to do. In fact, the count came that afternoon and was met at the station by Del Valle, Del Barrio, and Castillo. On the way to the hotel he was apprised of everything that had happened and his presence was immediately announced to the Empress.

They had a long talk together, and the next morning, October 8, they left the hotel arm in arm and took a carriage to the station, to board a train for Ancona where they embarked for Trieste. Before departing the Count of Flanders, who was a man of few words, briefly but warmly thanked us for our services to his sister and offered to send word to Castillo in Paris regarding her health and her journey to Miramar.

The Count del Valle went to Seville, where he established his residence and never returned to Mexico. The Von

Kuhachevichs traveled to Vienna, taking with them the Austrian and Italian servants. The Del Barrios proceeded to Paris. Castillo, after dismissing the Mexican servants and providing them with money sufficient to enable them to proceed to their own country, wanted me to accompany him to Paris, where it would not be long before we received news from the Emperor. He was certain that Maximilian, on hearing of Carlota's insanity, and being about to abdicate, would not delay in coming to Europe with the last of the French troops. He said, which was true, that the frigates *Elizabeth* and *Dandolo* had already sailed for Vera Cruz to bring the Emperor away.

I appreciated his suggestion, but told him that it was my duty to go to Mexico at once and that if, upon my arrival at Vera Cruz, I found that Maximilian had quit the country, I should come back to Europe on the same boat, under the protection of the British flag. So our party separated. I traveled to Paris by way of Civitavecchia, Florence, Milan, Switzerland, and the St. Gotthard Pass. I remained in Paris only a few days to rest, and from there proceeded to London and Southampton, where I took passage on the English steamship *Tasmanian*, which was due to sail on November 2. In Paris I received a telegram from Miramar, notifying me that all correspondence for the Emperor was directed in care of the Mexican consul in Southampton. I claimed it and sailed on the third at three o'clock in the afternoon, bound for Mexico where I was destined to witness scenes even more cruel and heartrending than those I had seen in Rome.

PART III
Querétaro

QUERÉTARO · I

1866

WHEN I landed at Vera Cruz the first person whom I met on the dock was Von Poliakovitz, who had left the Emperor's service and was bound for New York. He confirmed what I had been told by the consul general of Mexico in Havana: That the Emperor had left Mexico City for Vera Cruz, where the two Austrian frigates were anchored off Sacrificios Island; that he was still in Orizaba, where Generals Miramón and Márquez had gone on their recent return to the country. The ministers and the Council of State were also in Orizaba, having gone there to beg His Majesty not to desert them and to offer him men and resources to enable him to cope with the situation without the aid of the French, very few of whom then remained in Mexico.[20] Hence I was certain of finding Maximilian in Orizaba. I telegraphed to that city notice of my return, took the train to Paso del Macho and reached the imperial residence at nine o'clock on the following night.

According to his custom Maximilian had been in bed for an hour, so I waited until morning to present myself and receive his orders. I talked with Father Fischer, gave him the correspondence which I had brought and went to bed. A few days before my arrival, Dr. Bouslaveck had arrived by way of New York and given the Emperor a detailed account of the Empress' illness. The only persons with Maximilian were Fischer, who acted as his secretary; the Jewish doctor—Samuel Basch, the old naturalist Billimeck; his aide, Ormaechea, and the secretary of ceremonies, Don Fernando Magino. Grill was acting as valet and major-

domo; there were some Mexican servants. His escort was
composed of a squadron of Austrian Hussars, commanded
by Count von Kevenhüller, and Colonel Paulino Lamadrid's mounted gendarmes. None of the other close and
faithful friends of the Emperor were there; Bombelles was
in Paris, Shaffer, Günner, Hertzfeld, Eloin, and Scherzen-
lechner in Vienna; Dr. Semeleder had left to practice his
profession.

The Emperor received me at seven o'clock the next
morning. Father Fischer had told me that Maximilian had
been deeply affected by the details of Carlota's madness,
which had been communicated to him by Dr. Bouslaveck,
and warned me not to refer to it, unless I was questioned.
He was standing when I entered his room. I bowed, but he
came toward me, clasped my hand firmly and asked me a
multitude of questions about my journey, without saying a
word about the Empress. He added that within a few days
he would decide whether to remain in Mexico or return to
Europe, but regardless of what might happen to the Empire, I should always be with him. As we were talking I
had time to observe the stamp that so many emotions and
unfortunate happenings had left on his face. There were
none of the jokes and good humor of former days, and his
head, which before had been so proud and erect, was bowed,
as though by the weight of worries and sufferings.

His new adviser, Father Fischer, had recently come from
Rome, where he had gone to present the basis of the only
concordat which the Pope probably would accept. Fischer
was of German origin; he had been in the country since
1845, and had lived in Texas, California, and Durango. In
the last place he had been secretary to the bishop of the
diocese. Unfavorable accounts were given of the circumstances under which he had left this post. Later, Don Carlos Sánchez Navarro had become interested in him and pre-

DON TEODOSIO LARES

FATHER FISCHER

sented him to the Emperor who, being as impressionable as he was, soon placed complete trust in him. Consequently when Fischer returned from Rome he took the place of Hertzfeld as Maximilian's adviser. When I rejoined the Emperor Fischer had complete influence over him. The priest was tall, with a clear, ruddy complexion, he had an agreeable personality, he was always jolly, and had the faculty of promptly creating a favorable impression because of his geniality upon those with whom he came in contact. His influence with the Emperor was matched by that which he exerted upon the ministers, the councillors, and Generals Miramón and Márquez, especially the latter.[21]

With Fischer's aid the Conservative party had regained in the government the influence and the ascendancy it had almost completely lost, and during the conferences at Orizaba it decided the fate of Maximilian. The sessions began on November 25, in the Bringas house where the Emperor was staying. They were opened at ten o'clock by Maximilian, who was very plainly dressed and wore no decorations. Standing, he made a short address in which he said that he did not wish to take a definite decision [upon the question of retaining the throne] without previously deliberating with his councillors, wholly independent of French influence. He greeted each of those present and retired to his apartments.

The discussions were long and heated. While Maximilian's destiny was being debated and decided by the councillors under the influence of Fischer, he spent his time in the fields with Billimeck and Dr. Basch, collecting butterflies and insects, and remained almost entirely aloof from the action of the council, which may be said to have been preparing his end at Querétaro. A majority of the members decided that the Emperor should remain in the coun-

try and at once return to Mexico City. There were eighteen
of them, of whom four were ministers. The vote was eight
for abdication and ten in favor of sustaining the Empire.
Four of the ten were ministers, who had two votes each.

To attain the end which was proposed the ministers suggested raising a large sum of money, and Miramón and
Márquez offered to organize a large and strong army to
support the crumbling imperial cause.[22] In the matter
of the resources they could count on to sustain the fight
against the Juaristas without foreign aid, the vote was
very close, nine to nine. The President, Don Teodosio
Lares, who had two ballots, settled the matter in the affirmative. The Liberal opposition in the council energetically, and justly, opposed the suggested financial measures,
but the ministers replied that fifteen million pesos annually
could be obtained at once, which would meet the situation;
that they could muster thirty thousand men, of whom
eighteen thousand were then under arms. They added that
their calculations were made imperative by the immediate
situation and would prevent too violent a change of government, if a change became necessary.

Those who were loyal to Maximilian's interests were of
the opinion that the truth should be spoken frankly, that
they should make him realize the only thing for him to do
was to abdicate; that it was improper to compromise him
further, merely so his presence might serve as a safeguard
for the Mexicans who were seriously implicated with the
imperial cause. There were others who steadfastly insisted
that the situation was hopeless and that the Emperor
should be permitted to return to Europe. Among them
were Don Luis Robles Pezuela, Don Juan de Dios Peza,
and Don Francisco Somera.

The Emperor, for his part, took the position that he
should stay in Mexico, at the cost of any sacrifice; that it

would comport ill with his dignity to flee as part of the luggage of the departing French. Hence the decision of the council, which accorded with his ideas, was rendered in these terms:

"The Empire should continue to subsist.

"The Emperor should resign, if at this price he believed that the peace, independence and the interests of Mexico created by the erection of the throne would be guaranteed."

While the conferences in Orizaba were under way, Maximilian's effects, some of which had been loaded upon the *Elizabeth* and the *Dandolo*, were brought back from Vera Cruz.* That revealed his intention of remaining in Mexico, at all costs.[23] The result of the conferences was made public in the following proclamation, which was dictated to me by the Emperor, and corrected several times:

Mexicans: Circumstances of grave importance to the wellbeing of our country which had acquired greater force because of domestic misfortunes had convinced us that we should return to you the power which you confided in us.

Our state and ministerial council, convoked by us, are of the opinion that the welfare of Mexico demands that we should continue to retain power. We believe that we should accede to their desires and have at the same time announced to them our intention of convoking a national congress to which all parties may have access on the broadest and most liberal bases. This congress shall decide whether or not the Empire should continue, and if the decision is in the affirmative it will promulgate the laws which are vital to the consolidation of its political institutions. With this object our counsellors are now occupied in proposing opportune meas-

* They had been taken there in anticipation of his quitting the country.

ures and at the same time taking the requisite steps in order that all parties may coöperate on these bases.

In the meantime, Mexicans, counting upon all of you, without exclusion of any political color, we shall strengthen ourselves to continue with valor and constancy the task of regeneration that has been confided to your fellow citizen

Maximilian.

The Emperor's proposal to convoke the congress caused deep amazement among the councillors, who sought to dissuade him, but he insisted and stated that he would not alter a word of the proclamation. In the belief that when the time came to summon the congress it would not be able to meet, they ceased their opposition. Maximilian told me personally that if the congress decided against the Empire he would at once return to Europe.

Another motive that exercised a great influence in bringing him to decide to remain in Mexico was a letter he received during the conferences, which was written in Vienna and signed by his mother, the Archduchess Sophia.

In the letter she told Maximilian that the honor of the Hapsburgs would not permit him to leave Mexico upon the retirement of the French army, and that he should remain and await the outcome of the imperial cause, doubtful as it might be.

Eloin, who had gone from Vienna to Brussels, had written Maximilian another letter, dated September 17, which did not reach Maximilian until early in December, for reasons which I shall explain. Eloin addressed it in care of the Mexican consular agent in New York, perhaps without remembering that there were two consular agents there, one of the Republic and the other of the Empire. Unfortunately, the first received the letter and sent it to Juárez, who had it copied, showed the copy to M. Montholon, and then remitted it [the original] to Maximilian. I read the letter which, after referring to the retirement of the French troops and Maximilian's abdication, went on to say:

I am convinced that Your Majesty does not care to provide this satisfaction [by abdicating] to a policy that sooner or later will have to answer for the odiousness of its acts and the fatal consequences that will result. Once free from the pressure of foreign intervention, the Emperor should issue a call to the people of Mexico, asking for the material and financial support which is indispensable to the existence [of the Empire]. If this call is not answered, then the Emperor, having complied with his noble mission to the end, can return to Europe with all the prestige which attended his departure, and in the midst of important events that will not fail to arise, can assume the rôle which, from every point of view, is his.

When he finished reading this letter, after reflecting for a moment, Maximilian commented, as though he were talking to himself: "Perhaps I shall return to Europe soon."

The councillors and the ministers left Orizaba on December 2, but the Emperor chose to remain several days more, to take advantage of the climate, of which he was so fond, and which was beneficial to his impaired health. He continued his walks in the fields with the naturalist and the doctor. I had resumed my old post, despite the prophecies of Von Poliakovitz that, like many others whom the Emperor did not require to continue in his service, I would be dismissed. I had a room in the Bringas house and was summoned at all hours to take Maximilian's orders. As the post did not arrive daily our morning work began at seven o'clock, instead of four, as formerly.

After Hertzfeld left, the Emperor breakfasted alone. I ate dinner with him, for the old custom continued of all of his household joining him at that meal, with such guests as might be invited. We started for Puebla on December 12. It was a sad departure from Orizaba; the Emperor, sensitive to impressions, was palpably downcast by presentiments, fears, and anxieties, and especially by the insanity of Carlota, and seemed to divine that he would never return to the picturesque town which had so many memories for him and where he had spent such pleasant days.

We went through Perote, San Agustín del Palmar, the haciendas of Nopalucan and Ojo de Agua, and although everywhere Maximilian was still received with enthusiasm, no one hid his astonishment at seeing him again, for all imagined him to be on his way to Europe. Sensible persons, on seeing that he had come back, said that his presence would be, as it really turned out, a new cause of warfare, more sanguinary than before, and regarded with affectionate concern the unfortunate Hapsburg who was considered by those of judgment already to be the sacrificial victim of the Conservatives. At times when the Emperor and I were in his carriage, surrounded as he was by the troops who escorted him, it appeared to me as though we were prisoners, and I recalled the return of that other luckless sovereign, Louis XVI, who was captured at Varennes.

On our arrival at Puebla we took up residence in the bishop's attractive country house called Xonaca, which he placed at Maximilian's disposal. The Emperor refused to live in the city, and also thought of secluding himself outside the capital when he reached Mexico City.

QUERÉTARO · II

1866-1867

BESIDES those who had come with the Emperor from Orizaba to Puebla, our party was increased by two clerks whom I asked to assist me in my work, which was constantly becoming heavier. Because of the absence of Captain Pierron [who was in Mexico City] Father Fischer was the one who dealt with Maximilian in all delicate matters, and as the French [through Bazaine] on their retirement insisted on the abdication of the Emperor, General Castelnau, Napoleon's aide-de-camp, at Fischer's instance, had an interview with Maximilian at Xonaca. Dano, the French Minister, sought to talk with him on this delicate subject, but Maximilian was as reluctant to see him as he was Castelnau, and delayed receiving them on the plea of ill health. Finally he assented. Several interviews were held, which resulted in their being informed, through Fischer, that Maximilian required a month to think over the subject before he could give them a definite answer.[24]

Castelnau, realizing that his only object was to gain time, joined Dano in requesting another audience, which the Emperor granted. During it Maximilian formally announced his refusal to abdicate, explained his plans for maintaining the throne, spoke of his desire to convoke the congress and stated that if he relinquished power it would be only as the result of the desire of the body, expressed by a unanimous vote. At the conclusion of this interview the general and the minister returned to Mexico City.

With the exception of these conferences, nothing important happened during the two weeks of our stay at

Puebla. The Emperor went into the city only two or three times, but invited various notables of Puebla to visit him. His health seemed to improve a bit in the pure air of the country, and he appeared to feel less ill and at the same time more spirited.

Nevertheless, it was necessary to make ready for the coming conflict without further delay. We left Puebla on January 3, 1867, slept at San Martín, Río Frío, and Ayutla. At Mexicaltzingo, at nine o'clock on the sixth, everyone except Fischer, Billimeck, and Mangino, who continued on in a carriage, mounted horses and proceeded to the hacienda of La Teja, between Chapultepec and the present Paseo de la Reforma, where the Emperor established himself. On the way we were joined by a large number of carriages containing prominent persons, who acclaimed the Emperor enthusiastically. But close observation was not required to discern the complete lack of confidence prevailing among all social classes toward the imperial cause.

Maximilian was welcomed at the hacienda by the ministers, councillors, and high court officials who were waiting there to receive and congratulate him. His adjutants and aides had joined us at Mexicaltzingo.

We had not finished dinner when an officer of the mounted police came with a telegram for Colonel Lamadrid, marked "Most Urgent." Lamadrid asked permission of the Emperor to read it. It came from Cuernavaca and announced that scarcely had the Hussars ridden out of the city, leaving a small detachment of Mexican soldiers, when the place was assaulted by a force of Liberals and taken, despite the resistance of the Imperialists. In their zest for destruction the Liberals had sacked the imperial residence, the Borda house, and wrecked everything in it.

In his anger, Lamadrid asked leave to march his regiment to Cuernavaca at once and dislodge the Juaristas. The incident created a profound impression on those present, who asked themselves what would soon happen, if only sixty miles from the capital the Liberals were able to take possession of a city that had demonstrated so much sympathy for the imperial cause.

Another telegram came the next day, stating that Lamadrid's forces had driven the Liberals out of Cuernavaca and were in possession of the place, but that Lamadrid, after pursuing the enemy four miles from the town, had been ambushed while returning and killed as he was riding along slowly on his tired horse, with his bloody saber in his right hand. On receipt of the news the Emperor could not contain his grief or prevent tears from coming to his eyes. He had a strong affection for Lamadrid, and appreciated his loyalty and devotion to his person. Lamadrid was only thirty-five years of age, and was married to a beautiful woman from Sonora, who was living in Cuernavaca. Maximilian wrote her a warm letter of condolence.

During our stay at La Teja Maximilian rarely went into Mexico City. He frequently held meetings at the hacienda with his advisers. Various disagreeable incidents occurred as the result of letters exchanged between Bazaine and Lares. Márquez, who had been placed in command of the garrison of the capital, had levied a heavy tax and had pressed eight thousand men into the imperial ranks. Both measures created discontent and lack of confidence. Two still more serious events added to the already strained relations between Bazaine and the Empire, and led to an abrupt rupture. One was the arrest of Don Pedro Garay, a former minister of Juárez, despite a safe-conduct from the French which he carried; and the other proceeded from an article printed in *La Patria*, violently attacking the

French. The marshal demanded the arrest of the author
and of the editor and the closing of the paper's offices.
Lares did not accede to Bazaine's demands, and Bazaine
displayed his anger by complaining to Maximilian in a
long report in which he wrote, among other things:

"I have informed the president of the Council that in
future I desire to have no direct relations with the government of which he is president."

Maximilian replied, through Father Fischer, that:

"He cannot permit his ministers to be spoken of in the
terms employed in that letter and unless you deem it opportune to provide satisfaction for those terms, in future
he desires to have no direct relations with the marshal."

Captain Pierron, who with the permission of Bazaine
had been acting as head of the Emperor's secretariat in
the absence of Loysel, had been ordered to return to his
Zouave regiment. He was completely devoted to Maximilian, kept out of intrigues and without compromising
himself knew everything that was going on. It was arranged that I should visit Pierron in his quarters so that,
without committing anything to writing or showing himself at the imperial residences, he might confide to me information interesting to Maximilian, for me in turn to
transmit to the Emperor.

Pierron had a room in the Hotel Iturbide, which was
more like a barracks, owing to the presence of officers who
went there to arrange for their departure from the country. I would ride in from La Teja, leave my horse in the
patio of the hotel and go to Pierron's room. If he was
alone we would talk, but in case visitors were there we
would chat indifferently of various things, as though my
call was not important. He would present me as an old
friend, whom he had come to know in the Emperor's service; we would have a drink and when I left he would ac-

company me to the staircase and tell me what might be of concern to Maximilian. Thus Maximilian learned of the discord between Castelnau and Dano and also of the enmity of General Douay for Bazaine, whom he accused of enriching himself at the sacrifice of the honor of his country and of his troops.

During the last of January a serious occurrence required us to leave La Teja and take up our residence in the palace. We left ostensibly so that the Emperor might be in a position to deal with matters that demanded his immediate decision; but in reality because the police on guard at the hacienda had surprised two men in the gardens whom they arrested and who said they were thieves, although everyone supposed them to be Liberal spies or agents who had been commissioned to kill or abduct the Emperor.

An immense silent throng on February 5, 1867, witnessed the evacuation of the city by the French troops. Marshal Bazaine and General Castelnau marched at their head, to the sound of military music. Their flags fluttered in the chill morning air. The people, cold and indifferent, displayed neither hostility nor enthusiasm, although there was apparent a liking for the gay, elegant, and gallant Frenchmen who had fought victoriously all over the world, and also anxiety as to what would happen to the Empire when the French bayonets ceased to sustain its cause, which even the most credulous then regarded as lost.

The French were followed by a multitude of Mexican and French émigrés, employees, former ministers, generals, property owners, and others who, with justice, feared for their lives should the Republic triumph.

Another sentiment manifested by those who witnessed the departure of Bazaine and his troops was a certain amount of pity for the unhappy sovereign, who was left alone and abandoned to his fate, with a few thousand of the faithful, who having shared his prosperity would also participate in his misfortunes. The evacuation proceeded slowly.

Bazaine remained in Puebla over February 11 and 12 and on the thirteenth resumed his march to Orizaba. Before reaching there he heard of the defeat of Miramón [by the Liberals, in the north] and believing that this would exercise an influence upon the spirits of the Emperor, sent a special courier to Dano, saying that there was still time to save Maximilian, that he would wait for him in Orizaba and that from there they would leave for Europe. But Bazaine's courier passed another, despatched to Bazaine by Dano, informing him that on February 13 the Emperor had left the capital at the head of a portion of his army to carry on the war in the interior.

The French army was in Vera Cruz by the twenty-seventh [of February], and when the rest of the expeditionary corps embarked on the waiting boats, Bazaine went on board the *Sovereign* which, leaving on March 27, was the last to quit the shores of Mexico.

On its retirement the army destroyed a large quantity of projectiles and powder which it was unable to take with it. When Bazaine was reproached for not having turned them over to the Empire, he replied that, inasmuch as the Liberals entered the towns as soon as the French evacuated them, to leave the munitions intact would be equivalent to surrendering them to the enemy.[25]

Knowledge of this destruction, coupled with the rupture of relations between Bazaine and Maximilian and Napoleon's withdrawing his troops, contributed to the omission of the final act of courtesy, an official farewell, which might have been expected to have taken place, on the part of the Emperor and the marshal. In mute protest against the departure of the troops, the doors and windows of the palace remained tightly closed. Not a single person appeared on the balconies and even the sentinels were withdrawn inside.

But from the roof, behind a high parapet, overlooking Calle de la Moneda, toward the north, a tall man, wrapped in a gray cloak with a wide felt hat on his head, followed with his eyes the ranks of the French rear guard. When they had disappeared he turned to the group of gentlemen surrounding him and said:

"At last we are free!"

Miramón with a division had opened the campaign against the Liberals in the north with a brilliant triumph, the capture of Zacatecas. By a miracle Juárez and his ministers escaped, thanks to the speed of their horses which could not be overtaken by Miramón's jaded cavalry.

This victory was enthusiastically announced by the newspapers of the capital, as an augury of success for the Imperialists. But unfortunately six days later Miramón was completely routed at San Jacinto by Generals Escobedo and Treviño. He lost all of his cannon, etc., twenty-five thousand pesos, and more than five hundred prisoners, among them a hundred French who were executed. It was the receipt of this news, as I have said, that suggested to Bazaine to send his special courier to Dano, proposing that Maximilian should embark for Europe. It was not to be presumed that Maximilian, with his delicate feelings and his sense of dignity, would have abandoned his partisans at such a critical time.

Márquez had begun to fortify the capital in preparation for any emergency which might present itself. Maximilian, in uniform and with his escort, rode out every morning to visit the fortifications. In agreement with his generals, he was disposed to place himself at the head of the army and carry on the campaign in the interior. This decision, as he had reckoned, helped to raise the spirits of the troops, who had been discouraged by the defeat of Miramón. Some of the more timid of his advisers, like Father Fischer and others, who had not felt themselves safe far away from Maximilian or who were fearful of losing their influence over him, tried to dissuade him, but vainly. When preparations for leaving began, on February 10, the Emperor called me to his apartments and said:

"I am going into the field and no one knows to what dangers I shall be exposed. You are not a soldier and you are not obliged to follow me. Besides, you have a mother and brothers to support, and I should be very sorry if anything unfortunate happened to you, through any fault of mine. I should be glad to take you with me, but these considerations prevent me from doing it."

"Your Majesty has honored me by having me with you during your fortunate days," I replied. "I should regret very much to be separated from you when your days of hardship are beginning. My greatest sorrow would be to have Your Majesty leave me here and my greatest pleasure to be permitted to go with you."

"Very well," he said, "you go of your own will, and if anything unfortunate happens I shall not blame myself. On the other hand, I shall be glad to have you go with me. Besides being my secretary, you shall be my cashier and have charge of my expenses. I will give you some money which I shall get tonight from Sánchez Navarro. You may get ready to leave day after tomorrow, but say nothing about it."

All preparations were completed for our departure then, but at the last hour, late at night, the funds for the expedition were not available, so it was decided to delay until the next day, the thirteenth.

February, 1867

MAXIMILIAN left his apartments in the palace at six o'clock on the morning of the thirteenth and came down the staircase of honor to the main patio, where those of us who were to accompany him were already waiting: General Márquez, Don Manuel García Aguirre, Minister of Justice, Pradillo and Ormaechea—aides, Dr. Basch and I, with three servants, two foreign and one Mexican, and several grooms.

The Austrian infantry and Hussars were also there. At the appearance of His Majesty the officers surrounded him and earnestly asked permission to accompany him. They argued that they had come to the country only to serve him and not out of devotion to the Mexican nation, and that the troops of the Foreign Legion had not joined the French in their retirement because they were eager to save their Emperor or to die with him.

Maximilian was inflexible in his refusal to accede to their wishes. He told the officers that for the first time he was taking the field at the head of his army, in doing this it was necessary for him to have only Mexicans under his command, to provide them with a fresh proof of his confidence, and that he had made his decision and could not change it. He offered to summon them, when the campaign was under way, and assured the officers before they retired that he was infinitely appreciative of the loyalty of his valorous countrymen. Colonels Kodolich and Hammerstein and Count von Kevenhüller stayed by him until we set out.

We rode from the palace at seven o'clock. As Maximilian's intention to leave had been kept secret, we traversed the streets without the knowledge of most of the citizens, and only a few early risers saw the Emperor's party pass. At the northern roadhead the troops who were to go with us were ready. They consisted of two thousand infantrymen, the Empress' Regiment, commanded by Colonel Miguel López, the mounted Municipal Guard, with Lieutenant Colonel Díaz [not Porfirio Díaz] at its head, and Joaquín Rodríguez' regiment of infantry.

We breakfasted at Tlalnepantla, in the priest's house. At one table sat the Emperor, Minister Aguirre, General Márquez, Dr. Basch, and the priest, and at another, in a separate room, the aides and I. We drank to the success of the campaign in champagne.

A little beyond Tlalnepantla on the hacienda of Lechería, about twelve miles from the capital, we encountered the first Liberal guerrillas, who attacked our vanguard. Maximilian was not only serene during the skirmish, but took part in it, and after several hours of fighting the enemy retreated toward Cuautitlan, whence they were dislodged by Díaz' cavalry. A cornet was wounded and fell at the feet of the Emperor's horse. Dr. Basch attended him. I stayed close to Maximilian during the fight, believing that was the safest place, although bullets continually snapped about us like whiplashes.

The imperial troops enthusiastically paraded before the Emperor in Cuautitlan. In the plaza a horrible sight confronted us. An imperial soldier, probably one of the vanguard, was hanging head down from a tree, with his entire body hacked by machetes.

Before reaching the town a prisoner was brought before the Emperor, who had been discovered by one of the women camp followers hiding in a ditch, in water up to his neck. From him we ascertained that the force which had attacked us was commanded by Catarino Fragoso, who had three hundred well equipped and mounted men. Despite the protests of Márquez, who wanted the man shot, Maximilian ordered that he be incorporated into one of the cavalry regiments.

During dinner at Cuautitlan the Emperor was jovial and talkative. Evidently this life of action and danger had the effect of distracting him from the gloomy thoughts that had been tormenting him. Conversation naturally turned upon the events of the day and the Emperor congratulated me on the manner in which I had comported myself under my baptism of fire. Someone jestingly said that my bravery was due to the effect of the champagne of the curé of Tlalnepantla, and he was not altogether wrong.

General Vidaurri arrived at the conclusion of dinner, escorted by some of the Austrian Hussars, who had taken advantage of the opportunity to leave Mexico City and follow the Emperor, regardless of his order to the contrary. The escort was commanded by Captain Fürstenverster and Lieutenant Paulosky, who were delighted at the result of their stratagem, and asked permission to salute the Emperor. Vidaurri was also accompanied by Prince Salm-Salm, a Prussian, who after serving [with the Union army] during the Civil War in the United States had come to Mexico in search of other adventures.[26]

Like most men from the northern frontier, Vidaurri was tall and robust; he looked like a judge rather than a soldier. His Liberal ideas were well known but his adhesion to the imperial cause had created for him many enemies among the Liberals without winning him much sympathy from the Conservatives. Nevertheless Maximilian liked him, and counted on his name to attract many partisans from the Liberal ranks.

After a long conversation with Márquez and Vidaurri, the Emperor retired to rest from the fatigues of the first day's campaign. Our march the next day to Tepejí del Río was eventless. Mounted on his horse, Anteburro, the Emperor kept pace with the troops, occasionally galloping ahead for a distance and then returning to the column. I was mounted on a magnificent white horse, very spirited, and frequently dropped back to the rear to talk with some of the officers. When the Emperor summoned me I was compelled to gallop to him at full speed, and sometimes had trouble in controlling my lively horse. Maximilian rallied me, saying that secretaries were men of the pen and not of the sword, and that they ought to mount quiet mules rather than battle steeds. He put his idea into effect, for the next morning when we started for San Francisco the grooms brought me a mule, which they said the Emperor had ordered me to ride. There was nothing to do but obey. When he saw me he laughed and said that I was playing my part, and that on this beast it would be possible for him to dictate notes to me, which in fact he did.

This day's march was as uneventful as that of the day before. During the halts a house would be sought in which the Emperor might eat and rest, but if none was near his food was served under a tree, soldier-fashion, and blankets were spread for him to recline on. Our night at San Francisco was not so quiet, for word came to Márquez that a force of six hundred men, commanded by General José Cosio Pontones was preparing to attack us at a narrow place on the road, through which we had to pass.

We breakfasted at San Miguel Calpulalpan, celebrated in the history of our civil wars as the town where González Ortega defeated Miramón several years before. Because of the information received by Márquez, skirmishers were sent forward before we approached the defile. Fortunately, the enemy had taken possession of the heights only on one side of the road. Márquez decided to go by the other side, and open fire on the Liberals from there; this plan was severely criticized by some of the staff officers, for it would have been easy for us to have attacked them from the rear with part of our force, while the rest marched on through the defile. But Márquez persisted; our skirmishers opened fire against the Liberals on the left, who were protected by trees and who poured volley after volley on us. Maximilian rode in the van, with his staff. Our column was momentarily thrown into confusion by encountering a coach, drawn by twelve mules, which had been compelled to turn back by the fire directed on it by the Liberals, who evidently believed that the Emperor was riding in it. The frightened mules had overturned the coach, which blocked the road. This delayed us more than half an hour, before the coach was righted and got out of the way. While this was being done the Emperor with those who accompanied him was sheltered near a tree, and became a target for the enemies' bullets. Vidaurri and his aides pointed out to him the danger and begged him to take shelter behind a bit of rising ground.

"What do you want me to do, run away the first chance I get?" he demanded. "It is all right for me to expose myself a little."

We had almost reached the other extreme of the defile when we heard a tremendous explosion. Márquez had put a mountain gun in action against the Liberals. Maximilian turned his horse abruptly and galloped in the direction of the sound. We followed. Close to the gun, my horse reared and threw me. The Emperor came up and asked with concern: "Are you hurt?"

"No, sir."

"See, if you had kept to the mule you rode yesterday, this wouldn't have happened."

"Quite true, sir," I replied, laughing, "but in case of retreat, I could not have gone so fast as I could on a horse."

Three hours were required to pass through the defile and reach level ground. Some of the most resolute of the guerrillas followed, firing on us, but part of our cavalry charged with sabers, dispersed them and brought back several of their horses, leaving some of the Liberals dead on the field.

On our arrival that afternoon at Arroyo Zarco, in the tavern we found a good dinner that had been prepared for the Liberals, to which we did full justice, the more so because of the satisfaction it afforded us to consume food that had been intended for our enemies. On the following day, at 11 A.M. we reached the village of Soledad, where we were received with great demonstrations by the good people, who believed that an era of peace and happiness had begun.

On the seventeenth we advanced to San Juan del Río, by a forced march of sixty miles. There the Emperor had printed a proclamation to the army, which was widely distributed. In it he said that he had placed himself at the head of the army, in the ardent desire to fight for the two most sacred principles of the country: its independence and domestic peace. He announced that Márquez had been appointed chief-of-staff, and that the army had been divided into three corps, the first commanded by Miramón, the second by Márquez and the third by "the intrepid General Mejía." It was added that the arrival was momentarily expected of General Méndez, whose soldiers would form part of the second corps, and that General Vidaurri was accompanying him, for the purpose of organizing the troops as quickly as possible, to open the campaign in the north. The proclamation concluded:

"We trust in God, who protects and will protect Mexico, and we shall fight under the sacred invocation: Long live Independence!"

We were in Colorado on the eighteenth, and spent the

GENERAL MIRAMÓN   GENERAL TOMÁS MEJÍA

GENERAL MÁRQUEZ   GENERAL RAMÓN MÉNDEZ

night in that little town, six miles from Querétaro, and at nine o'clock on the nineteenth had our first sight of the fatal city where Maximilian was to be sacrificed, from the summit of the *Cuesta China* [China Hill]. There we halted, a mile and a half from the city, to spruce up a bit and prepare for our entry. The troops arranged themselves with what little equipment they had; Maximilian doffed his gray topcoat and white hat, put on a general's uniform, suspended about his neck the Grand Cordon of the Mexican Eagle, and exchanged his gentle Anteburro for the spirited Orispelo. We descended slowly from the mountain and reached the entrance of the city at 11:30, where we were met by Generals Miramón and Mejía, with their staffs.

It was a triumphal reception for the Emperor. For the entire distance to the Casino Español, where accommodations had been arranged for him, the streets were filled with cheering people. No doorway or balcony was without draperies and flags, and beautiful women who applauded and scattered flowers over the Emperor and his escort. In the main salon of the Casino greetings were extended to Maximilian by the prefect, General Escobar, and the civil and military functionaries. Accompanied by them, we proceeded to the cathedral, where a *Te Deum* was chanted. Afterwards a reception was held at the Casino, where Escobar and Miramón made speeches, which merited the strenuous applause they received.

Maximilian was too weary to attend the banquet in the afternoon. Márquez delivered a toast, in which he referred ironically to the youthful temerity of Miramón, in connection with his recent defeat. Although Miramón was pale with rage, he contented himself with offering a brief toast to the army. This rivalry between Márquez and Miramón, the two principal generals of the Empire, quickly produced results fatal to the cause.

General Méndez' brigade reached Querétaro the next afternoon at four o'clock, from Michoacán. It was composed of four thousand men, well armed and equipped. Maximilian met them, reviewed the troops and distributed decorations and medals to the officers and men. His Majesty, who appeared to have forgotten his fears and presentiments, presided over a banquet in the evening. Every appearance, at least, announced a new era of splendor for the Empire. Reality soon awakened the Imperialists from that golden dream.

March-April, 1867

OUR first days in Querétaro were quiet and uneventful. Maximilian rose at five, summoned me and we went over the documents which had been received, most of which contained requests for assistance. These were usually granted. After the Emperor had finished dictating letters, we would go about the city, often on foot. Maximilian, in civilian clothes, would stop to watch passing soldiers, mingle with the people or, as he was always smoking, ask a light from a passer-by or offer one to some gentleman. Other days he would ride, in charro costume, or in a plain blue uniform. Afterwards he would return to the Casino for breakfast and until dinner was served receive visits from the generals or the authorities. In accord with his old habit, there were always guests at dinner. He would retire at nine, at the conclusion of an hour at billiards.

There were nine thousand troops in Querétaro. Of the fifty thousand pesos that had been given him for household expenses, the Emperor retained only ten thousand, which since leaving Mexico City had been in my charge. The money was borne by two mules and was in the custody of two men I had confidence in and whom I never lost sight of. Maximilian had directed me to give each person of his household five pesos daily and two to each of the servants, besides what was necessary to the cook. My first care, when the siege began, was to lay in a supply of provisions for the Emperor's table. The forty thousand pesos, which was set aside for the troops, was soon exhausted. Orders had been sent to Mexico City to have the Austrian Hussars and Hammerstein's infantry bring more money to Querétaro, but as they had not been obeyed the Emperor was compelled to levy a forced loan on the city. This was covered promptly and cheerfully by the citizens, almost all of whom were sympathizers with the imperial cause.*

Campos had been appointed Finance Minister. He failed to concern himself with the Emperor or the army and eventually abandoned them. For this reason Vidaurri was named to the post, for it was of the highest importance at that critical time to economize to the last peso. Vidaurri complied with his task perfectly and paid the troops promptly. He placed the officers on half pay, but the soldiers received their daily allowance in full.

Maximilian displayed extraordinary activity, took part every day in the councils of the generals, visited barracks and hospitals, reviewed the troops and speedily became the idol of the army, which had absolute confidence in him and expected that his cause would soon triumph.

Before proceeding further, for the benefit of my readers, I will insert a description of Querétaro and its surroundings, written by the Liberal writer, Don Hilarión Frias y Soto:

"To the east of the city there are two roads, one cut on the side of the mountain called the Cuesta China and the other threading its way through a cañon, and hidden among rocks and trees. To the left of the first road, as it approaches the city, is a rocky amphitheatre, enclosing a level space, on the edge of which is a cemetery, with a wall which is prolonged to the walls of La Cruz church. Following the road one comes to the plaza of La Cruz. To the south of the convent [of La Cruz adjoining the church of that name] is the small church of San Francisco. To the

* Querétaro was, and is, one of the Catholic strongholds of Mexico.

west of the city, which is there bordered by the Alameda, is the Casa Blanca, a small country place situated on an eminence and extending as far toward the west as Cerro de las Campanas [the Hill of Bells]. The road from the cañon, to the east, winds in an ascending curve to the streets of the city. On its left, along a river that flows north-ward, are the poorer sections of the city. In front of the Cerro de las Campanas, and separated from it only by the river and a narrow strip of land where the village of San Sebastian stands, are the hills of La Cruz, San Gregorio, San Pablo and Trinidad, which form a chain to the east-ward as far as the mountain from which the aqueduct [which supplied water to the city] proceeds, and the Cuesta China. This is the scene where the imperial tragedy was to be played out."

Resuming the thread of my narrative: The Emperor one day collected at his table his old aides who were in Queré-taro with various commands. There were Colonel Joaquín Rodríguez and Commandants Ontivéros and Laurent, who had been dropped from the imperial household as the re-sult of palace intrigues. The first two, it will be recalled, brought from Miramar the documents concerning the ac-ceptance of the throne, and the last had been for some time connected with the palace. The company was completed by Pradillo and Ormaechea, the aides, Minister Aguirre, Dr. Basch and me.

During this family dinner we talked at length of the past, so full of hope and splendor, of the present, which was still promising, and of the uncertain future.

What was the state to which the power of the Empire had been reduced at that time? Throughout almost the en-tire country, the cities and towns had been occupied by the Liberals on their evacuation by the French. Only Queré-taro, Mexico City, Puebla, Orizaba, and Vera Cruz were held by the Imperialists. That was all of the vast expanse of national territory, from El Paso to Chiapas [on the Guatemalan border] that remained to the Emperor, and that was to help him in the difficult task of opposing the attack of the numerous Liberal forces.

Meanwhile the enemy was advancing from all points, which made it necessary to organize the defence of Queré-taro immediately. Escobedo was approaching by the road from San Luis Potosí and Corona from Acámbaro. The armies were separated by one hundred and fifty miles. Miramón, realizing the precarious situation, urged Maximilian to permit his attacking Escobedo. The imperial forces were almost equal to those of the Liberals. Miramón hoped by beating Escobedo and then promptly falling upon Corona to encourage the Imperialists by a first victory. He predicted, and very plausibly, because of his accurate knowledge, that this offered the only probability of salvation, and that it would be extremely difficult to win if the armies of Escobedo and Corona should unite.

But it was sufficient for a proposition merely to come from Miramón to have Márquez combat it. His influence was preponderant with Maximilian. So his opinion prevailed and we waited, completely inactive, and permitted Escobedo and Corona to peacefully effect a union. They began to encircle the city on March 6.

It had been decided at a council of war, presided over by Maximilian and composed of Generals Márquez, Miramón, Méndez, and Castillo, not to attack the enemy, but to give battle and wait for a chance to assume the offensive. It was also agreed to occupy certain positions [outside the city] with our right wing resting on the Río Blanco and the left on the Casa Blanca and the road from Celaya, with our center on the Cerro de las Campanas, and the reserves in the Alameda.

The Emperor, with his staff, rode out of the city on the morning of the sixth, at four o'clock. I followed Maximilian, who said that there was danger everywhere and that inasmuch as no one knew what might happen from one moment to another, it was best that I should always be with him. Day was breaking as we reached the foot of the Cerro de las Campanas. The fog was so dense that we could not see each other at a distance of two yards. But as the first rays of the sun dissipated the vapor we could see our troops in battle array and beyond them, a long way off, another extensive line of soldiers, whose bayonets gleamed in the rising sun. These were the Republican troops. Behind the Emperor we galloped along our entire line, to the sound of bugles and enthusiastic cries of: *Viva el Emperador!*

It cannot be doubted for a moment that, if it had been decided to attack the Liberals that day, such was the spirit and zest for combat of the imperial troops that the triumph would have been ours. The Emperor returned to the center, at the foot of the hill. Miramón insisted on attacking the Liberals at once. But Márquez opposed him, saying that it was better to remain on the defensive and wait for the enemy to attack, as had been decided.

Hence we did nothing all that day of the sixth of March, and at dusk our troops withdrew toward the city. General headquarters were established on the heights of the Cerro de las Campanas. That night Maximilian and his generals slept in the field, on beds improvised with blankets. I was permitted to sleep in the city. On my arrival at the hill very early the next morning trenches and parapets were being constructed. The soldiers cleared away the brush on the hill and its surroundings and leveled the surface. Those who lived near by cheerfully assisted in helping to place the cannon in position. I had with me the correspondence that had come the night before, and on seeing me the Emperor said: "Come to my office." Descending the north flank of the hill by a narrow path we came to a hollow in the rock, the entrance to which was hidden by brush and bushes. In the hollow was a seat of turf.

"What do you think of this office?" asked Maximilian, "Don't you think we can work here, without being bothered by anyone? I, Dr. Basch and Severo [the Mexican servant] are the only ones who know about this place, which I found yesterday." We sat down and I began to read the letters and note on the margin His Majesty's instructions, as we used to do during the good days at Chapultepec or Cuernavaca. Occasionally we would hear a shot in the distance, but little noise interrupted us, save the chirping of birds. Severo appeared at ten o'clock with a breakfast of roast turkey, cold meat, eggs, cheese, bread and a bottle of wine.

"Our breakfast isn't very abundant or fine," commented Maximilian, "but war is war. The open air will sharpen our appetites and make up for the quantity and quality of the food."

As a matter of fact, we breakfasted very well, spreading our tablecloth on the bank of turf. When he had finished, the Emperor lighted a cigar and lay down to rest on a plaid which had been brought by Severo, while he and I watched the enemy camp, of which we had an admirable view from the hollow.

Until March 12, while our general headquarters was on the hill, nothing of importance occurred that is worthy of mentioning. Now and then thirty or forty of our cavalry would ride out to defy the Liberals, who would send out similar parties. Insults and a few shots would be exchanged and both would retire to their ranks. In these little skirmishes the Liberals lost some men, including an officer, whose horse was brought to our camp. A council of war was held daily. The Emperor always wanted to attack, and the generals always opposed him. On the morning of the tenth, from the hill, we could see the entire Liberal army being reviewed for three hours; now and then the wind would carry to us the sound of their trumpets.

Because of these preparations, a deputation of generals, who feared that the Liberals would soon attack, asked the Emperor not to expose himself and to retire to the city; but Maximilian refused, saying that his place was where the greatest danger was. That night for the first time he did not sleep in the open air, but accepted a tent offered him by Mejía who, with Miramón, also had tents brought and set up on the crest of the hill where four months later the three were to die.

After the first few nights I also slept in the camp, since the Emperor feared that he would not be able to reach me at short notice—and with reason. The cold and the hardness of the ground did not bother me so much, but I was tortured by fleas from the time I lay down until morning.

Seeing that the enemy did not intend to attack and that important changes of position were being made by the Liberals, whose campfires decreased in number daily, it was decided to install the general headquarters in the convent of La Cruz, a massive colonial building, the thick walls of which made it a fort. We went there on March 13, the Emperor's unlucky day.

THE most notable incidents that occurred before we removed to La Cruz were:

On March 10 Colonel Quiroga made a sally and brought back two hundred steers.

On the eleventh the Liberals broke the aqueduct which supplied the city with water. From the heights of the hill we could see the cascade formed by the escaping water which fell from the damaged arches and flooded the plains. This caused a scarcity of water, but it did not lack completely, for there was still sufficient in the wells and cisterns.

At eleven o'clock on the morning of the eleventh, General Ramón Méndez, with the Empress' Regiment and another cavalry corps, made a reconnoissance in the direction of San Pablo. The enemy appeared on the hills and fired a volley and Méndez returned to camp.

At three o'clock on the eleventh, to test its guns, the battery on the Cerro de las Campanas first opened fire. In the distance we could see some riders fall, and after two or three more shots the cavalry retired, leaving the field strewn with corpses.

That night Miramón made a sally in the direction of La Cañada and brought to the camp more than sixty steers, a hundred goats and a great quantity of corn.

The Emperor had ordered me to keep a diary of the siege. Although it was lost when the Liberals occupied La Cruz, I retained a few very imperfect pencil notes. These, aided by my memory, enable me to reconstruct the diary, which I am now following.

In the convent the Emperor chose for his quarters a cell opening from one of the corridors of the cloister, which was divided into two parts. In the first was a table and two chairs and in the second his iron camp bed, which he always carried with him, a washstand, a clothes-rack and some more chairs. One door of the cell opened on the corridor and a smaller one, inside, communicated with another cell, with which it was connected by a passage. Maximilian had me settle myself in the latter, and I brought my bed and a table from the Casino. I had stored in my cell tins of preserves, provisions and wines which I had purchased for the imperial table. I also had a small valise containing the crosses and medals the Emperor had brought with him. Besides the door leading to the Emperor's cell, mine had one opening on the main corridor; whenever Maximilian summoned me, without going out into the cloister I could go to him by the little interior passage, which also served him when he came to my cell. Two aides, General Castillo and his staff, Prince Salm-Salm, Dr. Basch, and the Emperor's servants occupied adjoining cells. Only Severo, the Mexican servant, slept in the same room with His Majesty. All of our cells had windows overlooking a large patio, with trees, in which a battalion was quartered, and where the soldiers belonging to it rested during the day. The corridors, cells and passages were all occupied by officers and soldiers. It was almost impossible to sleep at night, between the constant "*Alertas*" of the sentinels and the rattle of arms when the guard was changed.

From the roofs and towers of the convent a great part of the enemy's camp could be seen perfectly. Their flags floated everywhere from the crests of the mountains and at night their numerous fires indicated their presence. On March 13, at 5:30 A.M. the Liberals opened artillery fire and projectiles rained on the convent. This lasted until 9 P.M.; during the entire day the shells exploded over the roofs. This belligerent announcement of a coming attack caused Maximilian, at 9 on the morning of the next day to visit the patio and address his troops. From our most advanced trenches observations were taken of the enemy's movements. While the Emperor was speaking, the artillery on the Cuesta China began to fire on the convent. Maximilian took his station and remained in the plaza [in front of the convent], which was a very perilous position, as shells were constantly falling close to him. There he received reports from the staffs of Generals Castillo and

Mejía. The first had been attacked at the Río Blanco and the second in the Alameda and at the Casa Blanca. Liberal onsets had been repulsed on three sides, and all the generals and other officers had fought bravely. Prince Salm-Salm, to whom the command of the Chasseurs had fallen when their colonel was wounded, made a brilliant charge and captured a cannon. This and many prisoners were our trophies. But on the La Cruz front the bombardment continued unceasingly. The cemetery had been occupied by the Liberals, together with the near-by chapel, and the Imperialists retreated to the inside patios [of the convent]. The danger increased momentarily. Márquez, with the battalion commanded by Colonel Juan Rodríguez, and supported by a piece of artillery served by General Arellano, sallied out and drove the Liberals back, after an hour of deadly fighting.

Then Maximilian, with Márquez and numerous staff officers, visited the lines, under the steady fire of the Liberal artillery, from Río Blanco to the Cerro de las Campanas. The Liberals evidently knew that the principal chiefs of the besieged army were in the group.

Although the fighting had been favorable to the Imperialists, it had cost many lives, and the Liberals continued to tighten the circle within which we were prisoned. Later it was officially announced that the Liberals had lost more than two thousand men.

By consulting my diary I find that nothing noteworthy occurred from the fifteenth to the twenty-first. The Emperor wished to make another sally and issued orders to Miramón, but for reasons approved by the council of war it did not take place. Maximilian decided to send Miramón to Mexico City in search of men and money. But, as always, Márquez objected and offered to go himself, arguing that Miramón's youthful valor and temerity would cause the project to fail.

Invested, as he was, by Maximilian with full powers and with the title of the Emperor's personal representative, Márquez was supposed to get together in Mexico City all the money and men he could find and immediately return to Querétaro, which was the temporary capital of the Empire. The abandonment of Mexico City would not have been important. What was necessary was to save the situation in the city where Maximilian was.

Although the intended departure of Márquez was kept secret, even most of the instructions given him being verbal, he carried a letter to the President of the Council, Don Teodosio Lares, accrediting him as personal representative of the Emperor. He also had a letter written in German from Dr. Basch to Lieutenant Colonel Shaffer, who should have returned from Europe, and others for Father Fischer. Besides Basch and me, those in the secret were Miramón, Mejía and Castillo.

As the situation was daily becoming more complicated, the Emperor told me that now was the time for me to return to Mexico City with Márquez and Vidaurri. I begged him to permit me to stay with him and share his fate.

In order to cover the departure of Márquez, at daylight on March 22 Miramón attacked San Juanico and Jacal, leaving the city by way of the Celaya entrance. At six o'clock the Emperor went to the hill and watched the operations from there. Miramón had two thousand men. He surprised and routed the Liberals, who left behind them in their flight provisions, equipment, and munitions. Miramón returned with twenty carts laden with food, sixty steers and more than two hundred goats and sheep.

Enraged by their losses, the Liberals retaliated with a

heavy artillery fire; they discharged as many as four hundred shots an hour. Most of the projectiles flew over our heads and buried themselves in the sand. Next day we had plenty of them, for we paid boys twenty-five centavos apiece for every shell they salvaged which could be used.

Márquez and Vidaurri at eleven o'clock that night with their staffs and twelve hundred cavalry succeeded in getting through the enemy's line without being discovered.

In the plaza of La Cruz there was a wide walk, running diagonally across the square. In the afternoons the Emperor would go there and while striding back and forth and taking his exercise would dictate to me the details of a new court ceremonial, which under the critical circumstances that prevailed seemed to me to be a truly ridiculous proceeding. Probably this was observed by watchers with field glasses from the Liberal trenches and the broken aqueduct, for as soon as he began to walk the plaza would become the target for artillery fire. But as the gunners aimed high the cannon balls would whiz over our heads and lodge in the walls of a house on the corner, which was riddled by the projectiles. Despite the pleas of the officers not to expose himself unnecessarily, Maximilian persisted in continuing to walk and dictate. One afternoon Miramón spoke to him very energetically of the uselessness of that temerity, in an endeavor to bring him to see the difference between being killed ingloriously if the aim of the Liberal gunners should improve, and falling on the battlefield. This had its effect and the Emperor ceased his walks, and the work on the court ceremonial was interrupted.

Everything was quiet up to the twenty-third and we believed that the Liberals would suspend their attacks, owing to the discouragement resulting from the setback they had sustained on the fourteenth, which would give Márquez time to bring up his reinforcements. But we were mistaken, for on the twenty-fourth, at 4 A.M. we began to see strong forces moving toward the Alameda, on the south of the city, while other columns advanced from the Cuesta China, the enemy's line extending from the hill of Cimatario to the Pueblito gate. The object of this movement was to cut off all communication with Mexico City and to encircle the town completely.

When the Liberals came within range of our artillery it opened a heavy fire. The resistance of Miramón's division was instantaneously successful, but Mejía's command hesitated a little, under the galling and destructive fire of the Liberals, until the general himself took the lead, crying: "This is the way a man dies!" and ran toward the enemy alone. Electrified by his bravery, his troops dashed after him, beat back the Liberals, and captured four hundred prisoners, including fourteen officers and a flag, and killing and wounding many. During the following days the Liberals contented themselves with bombarding La Cruz in the afternoon and at night.

Food began to be scarce, especially meat and corn. Horse and mule flesh supplied the former. One day while we were at dinner an orderly came from Miramón, bringing a fine pie. It was delicious, and we were enjoying it when the general appeared and asked us how we liked it. We all answered that it was excellent and he remarked: "When you want another one, there are still plenty of cats at my place, so you will never lack pies such as the one you are eating." The Emperor enjoyed the joke, for he knew what was in the pie and had touched none of it, excepting the crust.

On March 30 Maximilian organized a military celebration in the plaza of La Cruz. He stood under a tent decorated with flags and flowers and to martial music and the roar of cannon bestowed decorations and medals on the officers and soldiers who had distinguished themselves in the recent fighting. When he had finished, Miramón approached and in a short and affecting speech asked permission to confer upon him one of the medals of copper given to the privates for bravery. Maximilian was deeply moved and embraced Miramón after the general had affixed the medal to his uniform, and expressed his thanks. The troops cheered him uproariously and enthusiastically. To the day that he was made prisoner the Emperor wore the medal constantly.

From then until April 11 the siege progressed uneventfully, except for a sally by Miramón with a thousand cavalry, during which Commandant Pittner captured two cannons. Nevertheless the situation grew worse daily. Food was terribly short and we began to lack munitions. Fortunately General Ramírez de Arellano established a powder factory in the Carmen convent, where paper-covered cartridges were made, together with cannon balls, shells cast from the metal of the church bells and bullets moulded of lead from the roofing of the theatre.

On the anniversary of Maximilian's ascending the throne, April 10, a commission headed by Minister Aguirre and composed of the principal officials and functionaries of the city came to La Cruz to congratulate him and proffer their best wishes for the success of his cause, which then every one knew to be lost.

Miramón on the eleventh attempted to capture the head of the road from the capital, with the Chasseurs, and the second battalion of Méndez' brigade, commanded by Colonel Ceballos. They advanced in face of a destructive fire and after an hour's fighting were compelled to retreat. Enormous losses were sustained, and several officers were wounded, including Commandant Pittner.

In the absence of news from Márquez, fears and dis-

couragement increased daily. Couriers sent out with letters
or verbal orders for Márquez would appear the next day
over the Liberal trenches, hanging to poles with a placard
bearing in large letters the legend:

"THE EMPEROR'S COURIER."

It was difficult to find anyone with sufficient daring to
serve as a courier to Mexico City. Consideration was given
to a plan to employ Mejía's division in an effort to force a
passage through the Liberal lines and proceed to Mexico
City for aid. But besides the general's being ill there was
the question of who would have been left to hold Querétaro
if he had gone out with a division. The garrison had been
reduced to seven thousand men. The Liberals had forty
thousand. Prince Salm-Salm volunteered, with Major
Malbourg, to make the attempt, with cavalry support, but
the terrain was impracticable, being crisscrossed with
ditches, and after two hours' fighting the effort was halted.

Batteries had been posted at La Cruz, and on April 24
at 11 A.M. they began to fire on the Liberal trenches, at the
head of the Mexico City road. The enemy's reply was
hotter than ours. At the height of the bombardment the
Emperor ascended to the tower of the convent, with
Salm-Salm, Colonel López, Miramón, and Major Malbourg. While he was there, an exploding shell covered
them with mortar and fragments of masonry. That day
came near being the last one of the Emperor's life and of
the siege.

To hearten the troops, on April 26 orders were given to
ring the church bells and to circulate false reports that
Márquez would attack the Liberals in the rear, while we
would fall on their front. General Méndez on the following
day assailed the Liberal position on the Mexico City road,

the vanguard being commanded by General Pantaleón Moret. Miramón directed the operation from the slope of Cimatario. From the first the result was most brilliant, and the imperial troops demonstrated their valor by taking the first parallel in less than an hour, with twenty-one cannon and more than five hundred prisoners.

On being informed of the result Maximilian galloped to the scene. But in the enthusiasm with which he was received by the soldiers the object of the sally, which was to open a way out of the city, was forgotten. Since four o'clock in the morning the Emperor's effects had been packed and the horses of his escort saddled, but advantage was not taken of the enemy's panic and the opportunity for salvation was lost. I talked later with Liberal officers who had been captured that day, and they told me that the dismay among their men had attained a point which would have rendered it possible for us to have got away from Querétaro with our entire army.

But precious time was wasted in cheering over the victory. This afforded the Liberals opportunity for protecting the hill of Cimatario with fresh troops. Miramón essayed a second attack, but this time the Liberals answered with a withering fire, forcing him to retreat. So at one o'clock in the afternoon our troops returned to the city; despite the cannon and the prisoners they had taken the day had been lost. We were completely disillusioned with respect to the assistance that had been expected from Márquez and we were also certain that another chance would not be provided to escape from the Liberal cordon about the city.

May, 1867

THE events of May first were unfavorable to the troops of the Empire. A sally to the south was attempted, and after a heavy bombardment of the hacienda of Callejas, our column occupied the factory on the hacienda and then tried to capture the roadhead. The Imperialists were repulsed, and hurriedly retreated toward the city, fearing pursuit by the Liberals who fortunately remained in their positions.

While I was at the doorway of the convent that morning, watching the passage of General Severo del Castillo's column, I was approached by Colonel Joaquín Rodríguez who, it will be recalled, was commissioned by the Emperor at Miramar, and was with his household in Mexico City. During the early months of the Empire, he had lost his post as the result of palace intrigues. He had been placed in command of the Municipal Guard of infantry. At the time of the siege he was twenty-six years of age, with blonde, curly hair, clear eyes, of gallant bearing, very brave, very enthusiastic and full of ambition and hope. He was about to marry a beautiful young Mexican woman, when he was detailed to lead his battalion to Querétaro.

He seemed downcast this morning. Since I became acquainted with him in the palace we had been intimate. He, who was always good humored and gay, told me as we stood at the convent entrance that he had awakened in low spirits and that he had a presentiment that something serious was about to happen to him. I did my best to cheer him up. Before leaving to take part in the assault he embraced me warmly and said good-by to me, very much moved, as though he had a feeling that we should not see each other again.

Less than an hour elapsed. I was still at the doorway, listening to the sound of the fighting, when I saw coming toward La Cruz a group of soldiers, leading a horse by the bridle. A man's body lay across the saddle. It was Rodríguez, who had been killed early in the battle. Profoundly affected, I informed the Emperor, who was also deeply moved and ordered that Rodríguez should be buried the next day with all the honors due his rank and valor. Maximilian headed the funeral procession and the body was interred in the convent church.

Another attack was planned for the morning of the third, by columns commanded by Del Castillo and Miramón. The first was to simulate a sally at daybreak toward the hacienda of Callejas, the second to attack on the line to the north. But Del Castillo was delayed and Miramón, without waiting to hear from his column the fire which he expected, at the appointed hour proceeded with a vigorous and successful onslaught on the Liberals' advance lines and took the hill of San Gregorio. Liberal reinforcements compelled Miramón to fall back into the city. The Municipal Guard, who two days before had witnessed the death of Colonel Rodríguez, lost their new commander, Colonel Sosa, named the night before, and Lieutenant Colonel Daniel Franco, who was placed in command during the battle. Still the Liberals lost heavily—more than two hundred men, including thirteen officers.

To overcome the discouraging effect of this bloody day, false notices were given out that a sergeant, Guadalupe Victoria, had arrived at Querétaro with official despatches from Márquez, stating that he was coming with various corps. Even the designations of these corps and the names

COUNT VON BOMBELLES

COLONEL RODRÍGUEZ

of their officers were included. Although the bells were again rung and dianas [calls of victory or rejoicing] were trumpeted at the barracks, very few persons in the city believed the news.

May fifth, the anniversary of the victory over the French at Puebla [a national holiday], passed uneventfully. But at night the Liberals fired musketry and cannon, illuminated their camp and discharged thousands of parti-colored rockets. We expected a general attack and prepared to repulse it, but after three hours obscurity and silence enveloped the Liberal camp.

Pedro Sauto, a young man connected with a well-to-do family of Querétaro which was much attached to the imperial cause, presented himself to the Emperor one morning, and offered to carry verbal orders to Márquez. Maximilian accepted his services, and he started out, with nothing to identify him except credentials which were written on a small piece of silk paper. Sauto got into the Liberal lines by waving a white handkerchief, and was conducted to headquarters. Like the rest of the couriers who had preceded him, the next day his body appeared, hanging from a pole and displaying the usual notice:

"THE EMPEROR'S COURIER."

We learned later from Republican prisoners that he had informed officers at headquarters that the hardships suffered by the citizens of the city and the increasing scarcity of food had determined him to leave and offer his services to the Liberals. He was placed with a command and his civilian clothes were changed for a uniform. But while he was dressing, the officer who gave him the uniform found his credentials hidden under the silk band of his felt hat. The general in command was notified and ordered that

Sauto immediately be shot and his body displayed on a pole in front of the imperial trenches, to indicate to Maximilian's partisans the fate they might expect.

Maximilian was breakfasting alone with his physician one day, while some of us, including myself, were eating in one of the corridors. As neither he nor those about him lacked bread, owing to the fact that the nuns of the convent had plenty of flour, and sufficient bread was provided for the use of the Emperor and his household, I distributed what remained among my officer friends. Among these was Colonel Loaeza, who came into the corridor where we were consuming preserved fish and bread, because we did not care to risk eating horse or mule flesh.

I offered him some bread and fish and a glass of wine. Loaeza, who was a jovial fellow, referred to his breakfast as "the feast of Belshazzar." Heavy firing was going on, and Loaeza announced his intention of proceeding to the roof to see what the music was all about. Because of his gayety he had numerous friends among those about the Emperor and among the officers who, by reason of his stature and his always wearing big boots and full uniform, called him "Napoleon the Little." He had scarcely reached the roof when we heard a cry, and a few moments later two soldiers came, carrying him in their arms. A shell had exploded at his feet and shattered both legs. Hearing his groans, the Emperor came. Dr. Basch amputated his legs and later he was carried on a cot to the house where he lived with his young wife and an infant son.

Maximilian directed me to visit him the next day and I found him in his usual good spirits. He said that he hoped that the Emperor would not desert him, and that although he could no longer wear his big boots, he intended to devise a little cart in which he could get about and render some service in the army. I expressed the Emperor's regret at

his misfortune and interest in his condition, assured him
that if we got out of Querétaro he would always receive the
pay of a colonel, as though he were in active service, and
that Maximilian would send him some money for his expenses. Profoundly affected, Loaeza asked me to express
his gratitude to the Emperor and to tell him that if he died
he would die happily for having given his life for such a
noble and generous man. When I returned the next day I
was met by his wife, who sobbingly told me that he had
just died.

Among the Liberal prisoners in La Cruz were many
young men of good Mexican families. Several of them had
been mortally wounded, and Maximilian daily passed by
their cells and arranged for their care. He also visited the
hospitals and saw to it that the Imperialists and Liberals
were treated alike. When I told him of the family of which
one of the wounded—Castañeda y Nájera—was a member,
he at once directed Dr. Basch to attend him and asked that
he be provided with the best food. He had been picked up
before the hill of Cimatario, with eight lance wounds.
Thanks to his age and natural vigor and the care he received he recovered.

The other officers, who feared that they would be shot,
continually asked me what the Emperor intended to do
with them. I was able to assure them, because I was well
aware of it, that none of them would be executed, despite
the fact that our couriers were always shot when they were
captured. Castañeda was a colonel and aide-de-camp of
General Escobedo.

For several days after May 5 nothing eventful occurred, although the Liberals continued to bombard the
city, damaging buildings and killing peaceful citizens.

Discouragement and doubt grew daily among the imperial troops. No one believed that aid would come from

Márquez. Money and food were giving out, and desertions increased, even from the Empress' Regiment, which was one of the most loyal.

In the midst of that gloomy scene Maximilian alone preserved his serenity and his hopes: hopes without foundation, but he awaited his fate impassively.

It had been decided to break the siege; everything done in the way of planning by the councils of war had no object other than that. Wooden bridges, intended to be used in scaling the Liberal entrenchments, were constructed. Mejía called all the citizens of Querétaro to arms; they adored him, but despite this only two hundred men responded. The intention was to have this improvised garrison cover our retirement, if our attempt at getting out should result disastrously.

The generals on May 14 sent a proclamation to the Emperor, in which they included serious charges against Márquez. They proposed to attack the Liberals immediately along their entire line, and, in case of a repulse, to evacuate the city and end the siege at all costs, after putting the artillery out of commission and destroying what supplies we could not take with us.[27]

But another important question presented itself: What road should we take and where should we go, after leaving the city? With insufficient and demoralized troops it was impossible to make for Mexico City. At the first encounter with the Republicans we would undoubtedly have been cut to pieces. Our only hope lay in gaining the mountains, a few miles from Querétaro where the people belonged to Mejía, body and soul. There, with the aid of the valiant Indian supporters of Mejía and safe from any treason, Maximilian and those who were loyal to him might await developments. The final plans for the evacuation provided that Maximilian's escort should be formed by Prince Salm-

Salm, with the forces of Colonel Campos and the Austrian
Hussars; a battalion of the Mexican Chasseurs, the Fourth
Cavalry, and a squadron of the Empress' Regiment,
headed by Colonel López.

Maximilian also was to be accompanied by Count
Pachta, Baron Malbourg, and Captain Pittner. At a
council of war, held at eleven o'clock on the night of May
13, it was decided to leave at 3 A.M. on the fifteenth.
Everything was ready. Maximilian was not only hopeful
but certain that on the day set we should be out of Querétaro.

NOT only in Querétaro, but in the Liberal camp complete
silence and darkness prevailed on the night of May 14–15.
Not a shot or a cry of alarm was heard. On the previous
day I had been given five thousand pesos, the product of
the last contributions levied on the luckless citizens of
Querétaro. This sum was almost entirely in currency of
small denominations, and several times I asked the Emperor what he was going to do with it. In the afternoon he
summoned Lieutenant Colonel Díaz, in order to have the
money distributed among the cavalry of his Municipal
Guard. Our horses were ready for the departure. Maximilian ordered me to get together what gold I had and
portion it between him, Dr. Basch, Prince Salm-Salm,
Pradillo, and myself; and to give some silver money to the
servants. I handed twenty ounces in gold to the Emperor,
and to each member of his household; and to the servants,
Grill, Tudos, and Severo, 150 pesos apiece in silver. We
placed our gold in leather money-belts.

I finished sharing out the money at 10:30 P.M. Colonel
López came to my room and said that the Emperor had
ordered that some money be given him. I replied that he
had not come in time, that I had no money to distribute,

except a hundred pesos in silver. Angrily and violently he asked why I had not saved part of the gold for him. I told him that his name had not been on the list furnished me by the Emperor, and that I had nothing but a hundred silver pesos for him. Nothing was left for him to do but to accept it, which he did and went away.

At this time a council of war was under way in Maximilian's cell. I do not know what took place; I was only informed that the departure had been postponed until the next night. This was communicated to me by the Emperor, who told me that I might go to bed.

On the afternoon of the fourteenth I visited my friend, Castañeda y Nájera. Without telling him about the projected flight from Querétaro, I expressed my fears and doubts as to the fatal catastrophe that might end the adventure at any moment, and told him that my money was deposited in the house of Don Carlos Rubio. It included my salary for four months and my expense allowance. I asked him to get the money and, as he naturally would go to Mexico City if the siege ended, to deliver it to my mother. I gave him the receipts, and we parted with an embrace, without knowing whether we should say *hasta luego* or *adiós* for eternity.

It was exactly four o'clock on the morning of the fifteenth when I heard rapid footsteps in the corridor. My door burst open noisily and someone I did not then recognize entered the room.

"Hurry and wake the Emperor!" he said. "La Cruz is in the hands of the enemy; the convent is surrounded by Liberals!"

I leaped from my bed, half dressed, lighted a candle, and then I saw that the man who was speaking to me was López' second in command, Lieutenant Colonel Yablonski. I ran immediately to Maximilian's cell. As I passed along the corridor I could see that the soldiers wore the uniform, gray with very tall shakos, of the *Supremos Poderes* [Supreme Powers, a Liberal regiment]. Almost all of them were tall men. They were on guard at the doors of the cells.

The Emperor was sleeping quietly. I told Severo to arouse him, which he did, but he still questioned the truth of what I said and began to dress very slowly. Then Yablonski came and implored him to hasten. While I ran to the quarters of General Castillo and his aide, Colonel Guzman, Severo flew to awaken Prince Salm-Salm and Pradillo.

Yablonski, on leaving the Emperor's cell, also came to notify Salm-Salm, and then went on to Basch's room. Basch, as he told me later, hurried out of his room and ordered his horse saddled, and then ran in search of Salm-Salm, whom he found fully dressed.

"What has happened?" asked Basch.

"Hurry up," responded the prince. "We are in the enemy's power. Tell Fürstenberter [captain of the Austrian staff] to have the hussars' horses saddled."

As the doctor transmitted this order he met Severo who said that the Emperor wanted him. Maximilian was ready, and said calmly:

"It is nothing; the enemy has got into the gardens. Get your pistol and follow me."

Basch went in search of his arms, which were with his saddle, and was made prisoner. Salm-Salm, Castillo, and I, with the rest of the Emperor's suite and the servants, surrounded Maximilian and descended the stairway. It was filled with Liberal soldiers, but in the confusion we were not recognized.

At the street door a sentinel cried: "*Atrás!*" [Back]. An officer who was leaning against the doorway gave us a glance and said to the sentinel: "*Déjalos pasar, son paisa-*

nos" [Let them pass, they are civilians]. In the obscurity, for it had not begun to get light, and by the dim rays of a lantern which hung at the portal of the convent, we could make out that the officer wore a blue linen blouse, that his skin was white, and that he had long blonde mustaches. Afterwards we found out that it was Colonel Rincon Gallardo. We were quite certain that he not only recognized the Emperor, but also the uniforms of the officers who accompanied him and the swords that showed from beneath their cloaks.

Did Rincon Gallardo try to save the Emperor? We all believed so, or at least that he did not care to assume the heavy responsibility of taking him prisoner.

We groped our way in the darkness across the plaza of La Cruz, where our horses were stabled in an inn that fronted the plaza. Pradillo ran ahead, saddled the Emperor's horse and his own and caught up with us in the next street.

"Sir, here is Your Majesty's horse," said Pradillo.

"Neither General Castillo nor any of the others have horses; we'll keep on walking," replied the Emperor. We proceeded on foot. Various imperial officers and soldiers joined us as we progressed, without knowing what was going on. Before reaching the main plaza we heard a horse galloping behind us and halted to see who was coming. It was López. He said to Maximilian:

"Sir, all is lost. The enemy is in La Cruz and will quickly occupy the city. But I have a perfectly safe place in which to hide Your Majesty."

"Hide me?" retorted Maximilian, heatedly. "Never! We'll keep on to the Cerro de las Campanas. Perhaps we'll find some of our troops still there."

We proceeded toward the hill. Our attention was especially attracted by the fact that López, instead of going with us, remounted his horse and rode off in the direction of La Cruz. Why did he not come with us? Later we knew why.

One of the officers who had joined us, Commandant Juan Ramírez, offered to ride ahead to the hill and notify Colonel Gayón, who was in command there, that the Liberals were in La Cruz and that His Majesty with some of his loyal officers was coming close behind.

Day was beginning to dawn when the group of fugitives left the city and crossed the plain toward the Cerro de las Campanas. We were nearly there when some servants and grooms caught up with us, with our horses, but Maximilian and all of us remained on foot. When the Liberals caught sight of us they opened fire. Some of the shells fell close. The hill was held by a few officers, a hundred infantry and four cannon. Soon after we got there we saw coming from the city a part of the Empress' Regiment with Lieutenant Colonel Pedro A. González at its head. Then came Count Pachta with a cavalry picket and finally General Mejía with some of his aides.

One of the officers told us that Miramón had been wounded on leaving his house. The Liberals continued to direct a brisk fire upon us. Their projectiles hurled stones from the trenches a few steps from us and cannon balls thudded within yards of the three hundred faithful who represented the last vestige of the imperial army. From the hill we could see thousands of the besiegers closing in on us. Now and then echoes came to us of the cries of the soldiers who filled the streets of Querétaro and the merry clangor of the bells in the steeples.

Maximilian handed me his letter case, containing his most private papers, and ordered me to burn them, together with my notes, which I immediately did in Colonel Gayón's tent, where we found a candle on a portmanteau near a bed. Captain Fürstenberter lighted it and I destroyed the papers.

In the meantime Maximilian said to Mejía and Castillo:

"Let us get on our horses and try to get through this chain of men who are hemming us in. If we cannot get out we can at least die in the attempt." The generals opposed him and replied:

"There is nothing to do but surrender."

Then Pradillo and another officer, who were chosen as spokesmen, went down the hill and toward the city, carrying a white flag, improvised of a lance and a sheet from Gayón's tent. The enemy's artillery ceased firing. Our troops leaped from the trenches and ran toward the Liberal camp, firing their muskets in the air. A group of Liberal officers came to the hill, headed by General Corona, to whom Maximilian surrendered.

The officers surrounded us. Maximilian was directed to mount his horse. With him in the lead and accompanied by the Liberals, we started to return to the city. But at the foot of the hill we met General Escobedo, to whom Maximilian delivered his sword. He asked to be taken through the outskirts of the city, instead of through the principal streets. His request was granted, and he was conducted to La Cruz and for the time being placed in his old quarters.

Maximilian rode his Anteburro. One of the grooms who came to the hill with Corona, among whose officers were Riva Palacios, Echagaray, Mirafuentes, and another whom I did not know, but who looked like an irregular, took the Emperor's charger, Orispelo, by the bridle. The guerrilla snatched the bridle from the groom and led the horse away. But a short distance off another man, of the same sort, demanded the horse. When the man who had it refused to relinquish his booty, the second without more argument shot and killed him and took the horse for himself. This

BENITO PABLO JUÁREZ

GENERAL ESCOBEDO

occurred within two yards of us and in the presence of all
the generals and officers who surrounded us. Many other
similar incidents took place at Querétaro that day.

On leaving La Cruz the Emperor had given me his fine
field glasses, which I was carrying at my side. The Russian
leather case bore the imperial cipher in gold and was attached to a strap of patent leather. I held the relic closely
to my breast, but when we entered the city a Yankee officer,
one of the many Americans in the Liberal army, put his
pistol to my chest and demanded the field glasses. I could
do nothing but let him have them.

On our entrance to the plaza of La Cruz, General Echagaray with other officers was detailed to receive the prisoners, who were coming from all directions. The general
made the officers dismount and turn over their arms, which
were deposited on the ground. Soldiers took their horses
and the prisoners were escorted to the church. When the
Emperor arrived he was led, as I have said, to his rooms in
the convent. With most of those who had been with the
Emperor, I too was led to the church. Mejía, Castillo, and
Salm-Salm were imprisoned somewhere else. Severo, Grill,
and Tudos were released by order of Escobedo.

In the church were more than six hundred prisoners,
seated on the altars, in the confessionals and on the benches.
We exchanged experiences. Many were smoking. Someone carelessly tossed the end of his cigarette on a belt full
of cartridges which was lying on the floor. An explosion
and panic followed. The guards fired on the prisoners who
ran toward the doors, killing some and wounding others,
despite their cries that no one was seeking to escape and
that there had been an accident. By luck a general slaughter was averted, for the general in command went so far as
to have cannon aimed at the interior of the church.

Escobedo visited Maximilian and asked him if he wished

to be joined by any of his suite and told him to designate the ones he wanted. The Emperor named Pradillo, Ormaechea, Dr. Basch, Prince Salm-Salm, Colonel Guzman, and me. Search was made for us, and when we presented ourselves to him he received us with a sad, kind smile, and said:

"I am satisfied that everything has passed without bloodshed. It is better that way."

The events which had taken place intensified the dysentery from which he had been suffering and he remained in bed for several days. When I returned to my room, which was to be my prison, it had been looted of everything; bed, the rest of the furniture, tins of preserves. Nothing remained but a few broken bottles on the floor. The boxes containing medals and decorations had been destroyed and the contents stolen.

The siege of Querétaro had ended, after a valiant resistance of seventy-two days offered by seven thousand Imperialists against forty thousand Liberals.

May-November, 1867

INSPIRED by curiosity more than by any other sentiment, on the afternoon of May 15 many Liberal officers, including General Vega, Colonel Smith and the Rincon Gallardo brothers, Pedro and José, visited the Emperor. After leaving him they told the other prisoners how they had been guided into La Cruz by López, of whom they spoke in the most contemptuous terms.

"Men like him serve when they are needed," they said, "but afterwards one kicks them out of the door."[28]

The captured generals, excepting those who had hidden themselves, were in a cell near Maximilian's. Miramón, who had been wounded when he left his house to go to the hill, was being treated there by Dr. Licea. The house was his prison.

Among the captives there was great uncertainty and worry over what would be done to them. But, considering the magnitude of the victory of the Liberals, which was more sweeping than even they had imagined it would be, it was not difficult to conceive that they would augment it by displaying clemency, especially as it was due principally to the treason of López, on which they had not counted. Mejía visited Maximilian at dusk. The Emperor said:

"I am ready for anything. I am finished."

"I too am ready," responded Mejía. "Your Majesty knows that I have never been afraid to die."

Because of his illness, which was growing worse, Maximilian succeeded in arranging for Dr. Basch and Grill and Severo to sleep in his cell.

We heard on the morning of the sixteenth that a decree had been posted on the street corners, warning the imperial officers who had not surrendered that unless they presented themselves at headquarters within twenty-four hours they would be shot. This had the effect of adding to the prisoners in La Cruz Generals Casanova, Escobar, Moret and Valdés, and Minister Aguirre. General Vélez, who had been in command of the prison, left for Mexico City and was replaced by General Echagaray.

As the Emperor continued ill, Dr. Basch asked his permission to consult the chief surgeon of the Liberal army, Dr. Rivadeneira, who examined him, and gave his opinion that his quarters should be changed. He informed Escobedo, and on the morning of the seventeenth Maximilian was transferred to the Teresita convent. The carriage in which he rode, accompanied by Echagaray, an aide and Basch, was escorted by cavalry. As the carriage passed López' house, which fronted on the plaza of La Cruz, a man came out wearing a general's uniform and a sombrero and carrying Maximilian's embroidered kepi, which he had left in his cell when he fled from the convent. What had López been doing in the Emperor's cell?

The rest of us in the Emperor's suite were also marched to Teresita, guarded by soldiers; we arrived first and, ranging ourselves at the entrance to the convent, uncovered as he appeared.

"No other monarch can boast of having a court like this," said Maximilian.

The streets through which we passed were deserted; the windows of the houses were tightly closed and the few persons whom we met looked at us sadly and compassionately. At the convent two rooms were assigned us, overlooking a large patio with some trees. The air at Teresita was better than at La Cruz, and we believed that the Emperor's health would improve there. Maximilian, Basch, and the two servants occupied one room and Aguirre, Castillo, and his aide Guzman, Salm-Salm, Pradillo, Ormaechea, and I the other. We made ourselves as comfortable as we could, providing ourselves with fiber mats to sleep on, etc. Maximilian directed us to purchase blankets to cover us during the cold nights.

When he was captured the gold which Basch had in his belt was taken from him, but as Maximilian, Pradillo, and I were not searched we retained ours and no one knew how much we had. Don Carlos Rubio, a wealthy business man of Querétaro, who owned the Hercules [cotton] factory, saw to it that the Emperor lacked nothing. It was he who sent him food during his entire imprisonment. The rest of us had to depend on what we received from Maximilian and what we were given by charitable women; otherwise we should have starved, for our jailers did not concern themselves with whether we had anything to eat or not.

Persons were allowed to visit us and came daily, many of whom we had not even known during the siege. But now they manifested much interest in us and, pitying our misfortune, each of them assumed the responsibility of looking after the welfare of a prisoner.

A list of prisoners was published and was headed by the name of "Emperor Maximilian," followed by the generals and other officers, according to their rank, and ending with Aguirre, Basch, and me. A few days later another list was issued, in which the Emperor was designated as "Ferdinand Maximilian, Archduke of Austria." On May 18 there were restored to the Emperor the two valises that had disappeared from his cell at La Cruz, and that contained some clothing and books, among the latter Caesar Cantú's *Universal History*, which I had bought for him in Querétaro. At eight o'clock that night Salm-Salm was taken away. This alarmed Pradillo, who thought that he would be shot. He found out in the Emperor's room that Basch had also been summoned. But Salm-Salm returned in an hour, saying that the authorities merely wanted to ascertain his nationality.

General Méndez was discovered on May 19, in his hiding place. A few days before the siege ended, Méndez had engaged in a wrangle with a hunchback tailor, who knew him well and who had insulted him. Méndez struck the tailor across the face with his whip. The tailor swore he would get even with him. The day of the occupation the tailor dogged Méndez to the house in which he took refuge. He informed the Liberals, but Méndez had secreted himself so cleverly that he remained undiscovered, although troops surrounded the block in which the house was situated. They were about to abandon the search, convinced that the tailor had deceived them or was mistaken. But some ground where the officers were searching gave way beneath their weight, and Méndez emerged, covered with dust and armed with a rifle.

When he was brought before Escobedo, Méndez' only request was that he be allowed to see Maximilian before being shot. This was permitted. The Emperor said to him: "You go in the vanguard, General. We shall soon follow you on the same road." A few hours later Méndez died as bravely as he had fought in life.[29]

Escobedo, accompanied by General Díaz de León and Colonel Villanueva, visited Maximilian that day. We were very anxious, for we supposed that as Méndez had just been shot, the Emperor was to meet the same fate. But after a long hour of worry, Escobedo and his companions went away, and the Emperor told us that the visit had been merely a formula of courtesy.

It was impossible for us to sleep at night, for the

garrison of the convent had been greatly increased, in consequence of a rumor that the Imperialist general, Olvera, was marching upon Querétaro to rescue Maximilian. The incessant cries of the two hundred sentinels about the convent did not permit us to obtain a moment's repose.

On the following day [May 20] we ascertained that Princess Salm-Salm had arrived in Querétaro from San Luis Potosí. She was young, beautiful, and intelligent, born in New York of French parentage, of the name of Leclerc. There she was married to the prince and followed him in all of his adventures. Full of romantic and noble sentiments she hurried back and forth between Querétaro and San Luis Potosí and, in her desire to save Maximilian at any cost, had pleaded personally with Juárez.

In Querétaro she endeavored to enable the Emperor to escape, and to manage by the use of gold what she was unable to accomplish by pleas.[30]

The day she reached Querétaro she had a long interview with Maximilian, whom she informed of the state of public sentiment in San Luis Potosí and of what was being said there concerning the siege of Mexico City and of Márquez' treason.

About this time another incident caused us three hours of anxiety. One morning Colonel Palacios, an aide of Escobedo, came with an order to take Maximilian before the commander-in-chief. Despite his extreme weakness, Maximilian arose and accompanied Palacios and Colonel Villanueva and Prince and Princess Salm-Salm to Escobedo's headquarters. As the Emperor went out the imprisoned officers stood at the doors of their cells to salute him, to which he responded with his usual affability. Three hours elapsed, and we heard the noise of the carriage which was bringing Maximilian back to the convent. It was then eight o'clock in the evening. The most pessimistic of us believed that he had gone the way of Méndez.

We immediately joined him. He told us that Escobedo had been very agreeable. Salm-Salm, who acted as spokesman, informed us that the Emperor had proposed to order that Vera Cruz and Mexico City be surrendered to the Liberals, to prevent further bloodshed, and that he be conducted to Vera Cruz and embarked, upon his promise never again to interfere in Mexican affairs. He also asked that the lives of all of the Imperialists be spared. It appeared that the Liberal government was disposed to accept his proposals. Colonel Villanueva, who was constantly in the princess' company, said that orders relative to all the prisoners would come from San Luis Potosí in a few days.

The Emperor, Salm-Salm, the generals, Pradillo, Ormaechea, Basch, and I were transferred from Teresita to the Capuchin convent on the afternoon of May 22. The first night there we were lodged in the burial crypts of the convent. The crypts were damp, dark, and gloomy; their walls were covered with the names of nuns who were buried in them. The Emperor, too, despite the delicate state of his health, slept among the graves. The next day we were given cells on the upper floor, which provided a view of a large patio in which orange trees were growing.

Several days of quiet passed. Maximilian walked with me under the orange trees, allowing his dreamy imagination, as usual, to devise plans for the future. He believed that the Liberal government would permit him to go to Europe. He said to me:

"You shall go with me, first to London. We'll stay there a year, have my papers brought from Miramar and write a history of my reign.[31] Then we shall go to Naples, and rent a house in one of the beautiful suburbs which surround the city, with a view of the landscape and the sea.

PRINCE SALM-SALM

PRINCESS SALM-SALM

On my yacht *Ondina,* with Basch, old Billimeck and four servants we'll make little voyages to the Greek archipelago, to Athens, to the coast of Turkey. Later I shall spend the rest of my life in the midst of the Adriatic, on my island La Croma. When time has calmed political passions and extinguished party hatred, if you want to return to Mexico I shall provide you with enough money with which to marry and live with your family. If not and you want to stay in Europe I shall find a good post for you in some legation."

An officer one afternoon notified him that his trial was about to begin and that from then on he would be kept strictly *incommunicado.* The same afternoon the generals and officers were taken to the Casino and the rest of us again to Teresita. From then, June 13, until the sixteenth I did not see Maximilian. We followed the trial from our prison in Teresita. Grill came one morning with an order from the Emperor to send him all the gold we had. At first we thought this was due to lack of confidence in us, but later we knew that it was all given to Princess Salm-Salm, whose efforts to liberate Maximilian were ceaseless. We also learned that she had offered large sums to two colonels who, once Maximilian was free, would themselves go to Europe; but nothing came of this plan, as the Prussian Minister, Baron von Magnus [Salm-Salm was a Prussian], did not care to compromise himself by signing the necessary drafts. Also, Maximilian declared that he would not attempt to escape unless Miramón and Mejía were included.

Von Magnus had arrived in Querétaro on June 5, with his secretary, Shaller; Hoorrick, the Belgian chargé d'affaires, and the lawyers who had been named by the Emperor to defend him, Don Mariano Riva Palacio and Don Rafael Martínez de la Torre.

The escape was planned for the third and then post-poned until the fifth. It failed because the guard, which had not been changed for three days, and almost all of whose members had been bribed, was unexpectedly relieved, while the two officers who were in the plot with the princess were replaced by others. There was no doubt that the con-spiracy had been discovered. The guard about the convent was doubled and an entire battalion of troops had been posted in the street outside. Eight officers, including Colonels Villanueva and Palacios [who, according to the princess, were implicated in the plan], had charge of the guard. At night, when the Emperor was sleeping, one of the officers would enter his cell, bearing a candle, to make certain that he had not fled.

On June 7 all the foreigners in Querétaro were ordered to leave immediately. On the eighth the subaltern officers were released. The other prisoners, ranking from captain to colonel, were sentenced to terms of from three to six years in various prisons. On the tenth the officers who were prisoners departed, leaving only the generals. Two days later, at eight o'clock in the morning, the Emperor was left alone in his cell. Miramón and Mejía were placed on trial, defended by four lawyers. Meanwhile Maximilian awaited his fate; and in the convent of the Capuchins he heard nothing during the entire day but the steps of the sentinels who were guarding him. The prosecuting attorney, Don Manuel Aspiroz, opened his case on June 13 by reading the indictment [against the two generals and the Em-peror]. He presented a medical certificate, stating that Maximilian was unable to leave his cell. In the afternoon Aspiroz notified the Emperor that he had been sentenced to death.[32]

ON June 16 I was in Teresita prison, with the generals

who had been brought back there after two or three days
in the Casino. Maximilian and Miramón and Mejía remained in the Capuchin convent. The death sentence was
to be carried out at three o'clock in the afternoon. At noon
an officer came to my room and told me to follow him, by
order of Escobedo. I was escorted to the Capuchin convent
by eight soldiers. As I traversed the streets I was saluted
from the balconies by several ladies of my acquaintance.
At the prison, an officer took me to Maximilian's cell. He
embraced me. I was unable to contain my emotion and
tears blinded my eyes. The Emperor, who was dressed in
black, was arranging his beard as I entered. I saw in his
eyes the same calm and gentle expression as in the days of
splendor, but now they were saddened. He had requested
Escobedo to permit me to come to him and write his last
letters—letters of farewell, one to the Princess Iturbide
and four to the ministers who, on his ruin, had fled like
cowards and from abroad tranquilly watched the result of
their detestable policy.

The last letter I wrote was directed to Don Carlos
Rubio. The Emperor asked him to supply the funds required to embalm his body and transport it to Europe; he
would be reimbursed by the House of Austria. The letter
read:

Don Carlos Rubio:
Being completely without money I write you with confidence, in order to obtain the sum necessary to execute my
last wish. This sum will be returned to you by my relatives in
Europe, whom I have named as my heirs.

Desiring that my body be taken to Europe near the Empress, I have confided this charge to my physician, Dr.
Basch. You will deliver to him the money required for the
embalming and transportation and for the return of my
servants to Europe. This loan will be repaid by my relatives,

through European houses designated by you, or by drafts sent to Mexico. The physician mentioned before will make these arrangements with you.

I thank you in advance for this favor which I shall owe to you, and send you my farewell salutations, and wishing you happiness, remain,

Yours,

MAXIMILIAN.

Querétaro,
June 16, 1867.

When the Emperor had finished dictating this, I copied it. The letter was left unsealed, for me to take to Basch. Maximilian signed it and initialed the notes, which I put in my pocket. When I had finished writing, I arose and went toward the Emperor. The cell was very narrow. The iron bed, a table, a washstand and two or three chairs comprised the furnishings of the Emperor's last habitation. At the doorway, and blocking passage with his outstretched legs, was a subaltern officer who seemed to make a virtue of the insolence and bad manners which he displayed toward the condemned man. Whenever the Emperor passed near the door he was obliged to step aside to avoid the man's legs. Close to us was Grill. He was weeping silently. I could not restrain my sobs.

"Why do you cry?" asked Maximilian. "We are all mortal and my turn has come. Don't you think that at this moment I need all my courage, and that your weeping may deprive me of it?

"I have learned that poor Carlota is dead, and because of this I go to my grave more tranquilly. She was my only remaining earthly tie, and now she is in Heaven."[33]

A few minutes later he said to me:

"I did not send for you to write these letters, for I could have dictated them to Dr. Basch, but to say good-by to you and to tell you, if you get away from here alive, to go to Vienna and present yourself to my family, to whom I have recommended you. In the codicil to my will I have left you a little remembrance."

Here Colonel Palacios, commander of the Nuevo León Battalion, who was the Emperor's custodian, and Lieutenant Colonel Margain entered. The Emperor thanked them for their attentions and handed them his last five gold pieces, stamped with his bust, to be distributed among the firing squad. Palacios and Margain left. For some moments I was alone with Maximilian, until an aide of Escobedo told me to retire. Then the Emperor gave me a little case which he had in his pocket, taking from it a few written sheets on which he wrote the date with a pencil. Twice he pressed me closely to his breast and I felt a tear drop on my hand. Unable to repress my sobs I hurried away and crossed the patios and the corridors of the convent, which were literally swarming with soldiers, without seeing anything or feeling anything but the infinite sorrow of the farewell. When I reached my cell I threw myself on my bed and wept like a child.

Two hours later an officer had sufficient compassion to tell me that the execution had been postponed until the nineteenth.

What was the reason for the delay? As was easy to presume, everyone believed that the numerous pleas in behalf of the Emperor had not been vain and that the Liberal government had relented and would pardon the three condemned men.

But all hopes were baseless. The lawyers for the accused were certain that two-and-a-half days would provide them with sufficient time in which to obtain a pardon, for otherwise they would never have consented to allow the terrible suspense of the prisoners to be prolonged.

But Maximilian, who had not the slightest expectation that he would escape death, employed the days in arranging matters which were close to his heart. His sole concern was for his friends, his family ties.[34] He wrote serenely and gently to everyone to whom he considered he owed affection or favors.

On settling his earthly affairs, he turned his thoughts to the welfare of his soul, and knelt before his confessor, Father Hilarión Frias y Soto, an ardent Liberal, who wrote in comment on this act: "That monarch was greater when he approached death than when he smiled majestically in his palace."[35]

Among others, Maximilian wrote this note to General Escobedo:

"I desire, if possible, that my body be delivered to Baron von Magnus and Dr. Basch, to be taken to Europe and that Señor von Magnus take charge of the embalming, transportation and other necessary details."

This was inscribed by Maximilian himself, in his usual firm writing. I did not see the Emperor after June 16, although I tried to continually. All of us prisoners continued to cling to every remnant of hope.

But on the morning of the nineteenth, at seven o'clock, the battalion of the Supremos Poderes on guard at the Teresita convent was relieved by a picket of cavalry, as it was to form the square on the Cerro de las Campanas. The silence of death reigned, not only in our prison, but throughout the city. For two hours we remained in mute dread, without exchanging a word. Finally we heard the roll of the drums and gay trumpet calls—the Supremos Poderes were marching back to the prison. We all hurried to the first officer who appeared.

"What has happened?"

"They were shot. Everything is over!"[36]

THE FIRING SQUAD

MONUMENTS TO MAXIMILIAN, MIRAMÓN,
AND MEJÍA

ERECTED ON THE SPOT WHERE THEY WERE SHOT

GRILL and Tudos, the only ones of the Emperor's retinue who were free, were also the only members of it who witnessed the execution. After some days we obtained the following details from them:

At dawn on June 19 a funereal silence filled the Emperor's cell, save for the sputtering of the candles on an improvised altar. When the flame of the tapers began to pale in the first rays of light the servants, pale and haggard from much weeping, heard the roll of the approaching Republican drums.

To the noise of the drums was added that of the trumpets of the troop of cavalry which arrived at the convent, mingled with that of the carriages in which the prisoners were to be conducted, and the measured tread of the infantry.

The Emperor, clad in black, rode in the first carriage, accompanied by a priest. The carriage was followed by his faithful servants, Grill and Tudos. Dr. Basch preferred not to go with him, in order to spare himself having to see him die.

As the carriage passed through the streets of the city, men and women in mourning, their handkerchiefs wet with tears, and smothering their sobs, might be seen everywhere, in doorways, windows and balconies.

On the plains between the city and the hill all the troops that were to take part in the execution were drawn up, the polished steel of their arms gleaming in the rising June sun. A blue and cloudless sky hung impassively over the impressive spectacle.

Maximilian descended from his carriage and looking at the sky with eyes as clear, blue, and serene as it was, he exclaimed:

"I wanted to die on a beautiful day like this!"

After wiping the sweat from his brow, he handed the

handkerchief and his white felt hat to Tudos, saying to him in Hungarian:

"Take this to my mother and tell her that my last thoughts were of her."

Tudos retired, weeping. The priest also withdrew, and on the hill which constituted the scaffold only three figures remained—Maximilian in the center, Miramón at his right and Mejía at his left.

And facing them, a young officer and a squad of soldiers.

The Emperor said a few words, expressing his wishes for the happiness of Mexico. Miramón also spoke. After some brief instants of sepulchral silence the command was heard, uttered by the officer in charge: "Fire!" The air was rent by a deafening detonation.[37]

Soon afterwards the Emperor's body was taken to the Capuchin convent and embalmed by the physicians charged with the task. It was then encoffined and placed in the entresol of the house of Señor Muñoz Ledo, which was the headquarters of the government. That day the Austrian minister asked that the body be delivered to him, but Juárez' foreign minister answered that there were serious reasons why the request could not be granted. A similar solicitation made ten days later by Baron von Magnus and Dr. Basch was also denied.

The Austrian frigate *Novara,* commanded by Vice Admiral Teghettoff, arrived at Vera Cruz on August 25. Early in September the Admiral presented himself to the foreign minister, saying that as a friend of the reigning family of Austria, with a purely confidential mission, he had come to ask that the body be delivered to him.

The minister replied that this could not be done, except by express request of the Austrian government or at least of Maximilian's family. Hence on September 26, Beust,

the Austrian Minister of the Imperial Household, despatched a note to the Austrian minister in Mexico, asking
him to obtain from President Juárez the delivery of the
body to Admiral Teghettoff. Juárez then ordered returned
to Austria the remains of him who, in the prime of life, had
been summoned to Mexico by a handful of Mexicans, in
the belief that he could save the country.

Almost five months after the execution of His Majesty,
at five o'clock on the morning of November 12, two vehi-
cles, escorted by three hundred troops, halted at the door
of the Hospital of San Andrés, in Mexico City. After a
short delay the coffin containing the Emperor's body was
brought out. On the same day, with its escort, it began the
journey to Vera Cruz, to be delivered to Admiral Teghettoff by his brother, Count Teghettoff; the Admiral's aides,
Von Gaal and Hennebig, and Dr. Basch.

The Admiral had succeeded in obtaining the release of
all the Austrian and Belgian prisoners, who sailed from
Mexico aboard the *Novara*. He officially received the body
and the keys of the coffin on November 25, at Vera Cruz.
On the following day it was placed in an improvised chapel
on the frigate.

Thus it happened that the same craft that three-and-a-
half years before had brought to Mexico two young sovereigns, laden with hopes and illusions, bore away the corpse
of one of them to deposit it, after a long voyage over several seas, in the crypt of the Capuchin convent in Vienna,
the final resting place of the members of the imperial house
of Hapsburg.

1867-1868

I was taken on July 1, under guard, from my prison in Teresita to General Escobedo's house. Almost all the prisoners had then been sent to various places to serve their sentences. There remained in Teresita only Minister Aguirre, a young clerk, Manuel Castillo, and I.

Escobedo asked me what had been my rank in the army. I told him that I had held no rank, and had accompanied the Emperor solely in the capacity of secretary. He inquired where I wanted to go in Mexico. I replied, to Mexico City. He gave me a passport and ordered me to report to Minister Lerdo de Tejada when I reached the capital. Two days later, with some money, a good horse, and accompanied by Grill and Tudos, I started for Mexico City. For protection against bandits we traveled behind a battalion of troops bound for the capital.

My family was greatly surprised to see me in the city, for they had received no news of me. My friend, Castañeda y Nájera, had delivered to my mother the money belonging to me which he had obtained in Querétaro. Early in November I started for Vienna, from Vera Cruz, on the French steamship *Panama*.

I found aboard Venisch, the Emperor's major-domo, and his family, and one of the grooms, Muller, also with his family; Baron von Magnus, the Prussian Minister; one of the Emperor's former ministers, Larrainzar, who was going into exile; and Eloin. Generals Castillo and Escobar and Prince Salm-Salm were prisoners in the fortress of Ulúa. The princess, although unable to save Maximilian, worked to obtain the release of her husband, which she finally succeeded in doing, on condition that he leave the country. Hence the prince also accompanied me on the voyage. For some reason unknown to me the princess remained in Vera Cruz. When we sailed on November 15 the steamship carried a large number of Austrians and Belgians who were returning to their countries.

I reached Vienna on January 8. A few days later I solicited an audience with Emperor Franz Joseph, which was immediately granted. Presenting my card of introduction at the palace, I was conducted by a chamberlain, through long galleries and splendid salons, guarded by soldiers in uniforms similar to those worn by the palace guard in Mexico, to a door flanked by two sentinels. My guide rapped lightly on the portal of the Emperor's office. We heard a voice say in German: "Come in." Franz Joseph, who was as tall as his brother Maximilian, was standing near a table on which were various papers, wearing the blue uniform of the Austrian cavalry, with a sword at his belt. His expression was reserved and severe and despite his resemblance to his brother, imposed respect without inviting one's sympathy, as did the kind countenance of the other. He asked me in German if I spoke that language and when I answered in the negative, he talked to me in very correct French. He asked me whether I had witnessed the siege of Querétaro, whether I had seen his brother die, when I had left Mexico, and if I desired to remain in Vienna and settle there. I replied in detail and said that I thought of spending two years in Europe and then returning to Mexico.

The Emperor requested me to talk with the Archduke Charles Louis, to whom Maximilian had written concerning his affairs, and said that if I decided to stay in Vienna to let him know if there was anything he could do for me.

The interview lasted for half an hour. A few days afterwards I was received by the Archduke Charles Louis in his
residence. Charles Louis looked more like his unfortunate
brother than Franz Joseph. After questioning me about
the siege and the death of Maximilian, he informed me that
the Emperor, believing that his effects in Mexico would be
turned over to his family by the government, had added a
codicil to his will providing that the proceeds of their sale
should be equally divided among Shaffer, Günner, Pradillo, Dr. Basch, and me. He had written, he said, to the
Minister of the Imperial Household, Sánchez Navarro,
who had informed him that not only had the government
confiscated the personal property of Maximilian, but that
Navarro himself had lost his personal fortune in the imperial cause. We who were mentioned in the codicil would
receive what might be realized from the sale of Maximilian's yacht, the *Ondina*, which was lying in the port of
Trieste, and which was not worth a great deal, although it
was equipped with very good marine instruments. The
Archduke added that the matter was in the hands of Dr.
Possony, the court attorney, to whom he gave me a letter,
and said that I should apply to him for details.

My third visit was made to Maximilian's mother, the
Archduchess Sophia. At that time she was in her sixties,
with pure white hair, which in accordance with the prevailing style was covered with a light cap of black silk lace. Her
gown was of dark silk. She indicated that I was to seat
myself near her.

"You are probably the young Mexican whom my son
Max mentioned in his letters," she said in French. "He told
me that you accompanied him everywhere, that you had
the habit of writing in the coach when you traveled and
that you are the one whom he made work at four o'clock in
the morning. My son praised you highly in his letters."

CONVENT OF LA CRUZ

MEMORIAL CHAPEL

ERECTED BY THE AUSTRIAN GOVERNMENT AT QUERÉTARO

"I had the good fortune to be distinguished by His Majesty with his confidence," I replied, "and with his affection, and I was very happy to serve him during three years of his reign."

On hearing the details which I gave her and also afterwards when I was answering her questions, the Archduchess wept several times. As she dried her eyes she may have recalled her responsibility in the death of her son, when in the letter from her which he received in Orizaba she almost compelled him to sustain the Empire to the end, instead of leaving Mexico with the French.

My audience lasted for an hour, and although I started to leave now and again the Archduchess would detain me to ask new questions or to hear me repeat some of the details I had given her before. When I finally took my leave, she requested me to come again, saying that although my story had caused her to suffer it had afforded her the consolation of hearing about her dear son Max from a person who had been with him daily and who had loved him so much.

A few days later I received another invitation to wait upon her. The appointment was for eleven o'clock and I was asked to remain for breakfast. While alone with her at the table I recalled the many times when I had been seated, almost familiarly, face to face with the Emperor of Mexico.

During my stay in Vienna the *Novara* arrived in Trieste with the Emperor's body. It was brought ashore on January 16, 1868, on a launch covered with black velvet. In the center of the craft was a catafalque, upon which the coffin rested, and at its prow an angel with outstretched wings, bearing a crown of laurel. On the poop the arms of the Mexican Empire were displayed, with the Mexican and the Austrian flags. The coffin was taken from the wharf to the railway station in a sumptuous funeral car. The entire city of Trieste was in mourning. The special train left Trieste at 1 P.M. and reached Vienna at eight o'clock the following evening. When the coffin was carried into the imperial palace it was covered with snow, which had been falling since afternoon. It was received at the entrance to the palace by the Archduchess Sophia and Maximilian's brothers. The Archduchess threw herself sobbing upon the coffin. On viewing through the glass the pallid, serene face of her favorite son, she knelt, and for several moments nothing could be heard but her broken sobs. At midnight the coffin was transferred to the imperial chapel. There it remained for a day and was viewed by the people of Vienna and its vicinity.

By a curious coincidence the remains of Maximilian, who had spent his last days in a Capuchin convent, found their final resting place in the crypt of the Capuchins of Vienna, where all the members of the Hapsburg dynasty rested. The body was taken there on the afternoon of January 20. An invitation had been sent me by the grand marshal of the court. Among those surrounding the coffin who had been connected with the Empire were Count Bombelles, Marquis von Corio, Major Günner,[38] Count von Kevenhüller, Eloin, Baron Malbourg, Dr. Basch, and Commandant Pittner, some of whom had been made prisoners at Querétaro. Don Hilarión Frias y Soto, who in referring to the Empire is an impartial critic, speaking of the ceremony says: "Not one Mexican came to those ceremonies. All the notables of the imperial court, the ministers, councilors and high functionaries of Maximilian were in Europe, where they had fled from the justice of the Republic, but not one of those men had gone to pay a tribute of homage to the Emperor who had lavished honor, gold and distinction upon them." He is telling the truth when he says that there were no Mexicans at the funeral services of the Emperor from among the imperial party who had received honors, gold, and distinctions from him, but he is quite wrong in saying that there was no Mexican present, since there were there Don Gregorio Barandiarán, the Minister in Vienna, his secretary, Don Ángel Núñez, and he who is writing these lines.

Some days after the funeral I received a letter, asking me to call at the Belgian legation. There I was given a photograph of Maximilian, showing him in sailor's uniform, standing at the prow of a vessel with a flag in his arms, in the midst of a stormy sea. On the wrapper of the photograph was written in Carlota's hand: "To Don José Luis Blasio," and below, in writing which I did not recognize: "Former Secretary of Emperor Maximilian. Vienna." I judged that the photograph had been taken from a painting, symbolical of the shipwreck of the Mexican Empire, which had been done by order of Carlota herself in one of her lucid intervals. It was evident that the Empress was not ignorant of Maximilian's tragic end, for on the back of the photograph was inscribed: "Pray for the repose of the soul of His Majesty, Ferdinand Maximilian Joseph, Emperor of Mexico. Born at Schoenbrunn, July 6, 1832. Died at Querétaro, June 19, 1867." This was followed by two verses from the Bible, in Latin and Spanish.

The receipt of the photograph intensified my desire to see the Empress. I proceeded to Brussels and solicited an audience with her. I was told that before it was granted her physicians would have to be consulted. After a few days I was informed that their decision was in the negative. They concluded that although my presence might produce a favorable effect on the Empress' mind, there was also a strong probability that it might lead to a fatal crisis. I was also told that in one of her lucid days Carlota had caused the painting to be made and photographed, and copies sent to Bombelles, Corio, Hidalgo [Maximilian's Minister in Paris, and one of the original promoters of the Empire], and other persons of the Emperor's court. Soon after she had done this, she again became irrational, and was now in that state.

Determined at least to see the château of Laeken, where she was living, I went there, and one afternoon, from the gate, I caught a glimpse of three ladies, walking under the old trees of the park, all dressed in mourning. On nearing the grating I recognized by her graceful figure the Empress Carlota between the other two ladies. She was strolling along slowly, dressed and groomed with extreme elegance and care. Her gentle and kind face was profoundly sad. Her large eyes, so black and beautiful, appeared even larger and more beautiful under their purple lids. But they stared vacantly, as though questioning her destiny. As the three ladies neared me, I was on the point of calling, "Señora, here is one of the most faithful servants of your Majesty who, on returning to his country, wishes to take with him the memory of having spoken perhaps for the last time with her who so often favored him with her orders, so often honored him with her words." But when they were near the grating, they turned and went slowly away among the trees. I left Brussels the next day.

During my subsequent stay in Vienna the *Ondina* was sold to a wealthy Turk, Jacob Munzi, for 11,502 florins. Dr. Possony paid me my share of this. Other property of Maximilian, worth fifty thousand florins, remained to be disposed of, but of this the persons named in his codicil received nothing.

Before I left Vienna I paid a final visit to the crypt of the Capuchins. The friar who guided me pointed out the

CARLOTA

IN 1926

sepulchers of the imperial family and in a measured tone
repeated the names of the illustrious dead:
"The Empress, Maria Theresa."
"His Majesty, Emperor Joseph II."
"The Duke of Reichstadt, son of Napoleon," and finally,
"Maximilian, Emperor of Mexico."
I knelt before his tomb.

*   *   *   *   *   *

*I have written these pages with no pretense at being a
historian or a littérateur, but with the sole desire that the
historical figure, whom so many have endeavored to slan-
der, might become better known. I have set down my remi-
niscences impartially, without passion or rancor. I have
also endeavored to inspire a sympathetic understanding of
the personage who, as a ruler, may have committed great
errors, but who, as a man, possessed the most noble, loyal
and the greatest heart that could exist.*

APPENDICES

Treaty of Miramar
Plans for Maximilian's Escape
Disposition of Maximilian's Body

APPENDICES · I

Treaty of Miramar

NAPOLEON, *by the grace of God and the national will Emperor of the French, to all to whom these presents may come, greeting:*

A convention, followed by secret additional articles having been concluded on April 10th, 1864, between France and Mexico, to settle the conditions of the sojourn of the French troops in Mexico, the said convention and secret additional articles are as follows:

The government of H. M. the Emperor of the French and that of H. M. the Emperor of Mexico, animated with an equal desire to assure the reëstablishment of order in Mexico and to consolidate the new Empire, have resolved to settle through a convention the conditions of the sojourn of the French troops in that country and have appointed to that effect Commissioners who, after communicating their full powers to one another, these having been found to be in good and due form, have agreed upon the following articles:

ARTICLE 1. The French troops actually in Mexico shall, so soon as possible, be reduced to a corps of 25,000 men, including the foreign legion. This corps as a safeguard to the interests which have brought about the French intervention shall temporarily remain in Mexico under the conditions agreed upon in the following articles.

ARTICLE 2. The French troops shall gradually evacuate Mexico as H. M. the Emperor of Mexico shall be able to reorganize the troops necessary to take their place.

ARTICLE 3. The foreign legion in the service of France, composed of 8,000 men, shall, however, remain in Mexico for six years after all other French troops have been recalled under Article 2. From that date the said legion shall pass into the service and pay of the Mexican government, the Mexican government reserving to itself the right to shorten the duration of the employment in Mexico of the foreign legion.

ARTICLE 4. The points of the territory to be occupied by the French troops, as well as the military expeditions of said troops if necessary, shall be determined under direct agreement between H. M. the Emperor of Mexico and the commander-in-chief of the French corps.

ARTICLE 5. Upon all points where a garrison shall not be composed exclusively of Mexican troops, the military command shall devolve upon the French commander. In case of combined expeditions of French and Mexican troops the superior command shall also belong to the French commander.

ARTICLE 6. The French commander shall not interfere with any branch of the Mexican administration.

ARTICLE 7. So long as the needs of the French army corps will require, every two months a service of transports between France and the port of Vera Cruz shall be maintained; the expense of this service, fixed at the sum of 400,000 francs per journey, including return, shall be borne by the Mexican government and paid in Mexico.

ARTICLE 8. The naval stations supported by France in the Antilles and in the Pacific Ocean shall frequently send ships to show the French flag in the Mexican ports.

ARTICLE 9. The cost of the French expedition to Mexico, to be reimbursed by the Mexican government, is fixed at the sum of 270,000,000 francs from the time of the expedition to July 1, 1864. This sum shall bear interest at 3 percent a year.

ARTICLE 10. The indemnity to be paid to France by the Mexican government for the pay and support of the army corps from July 1, 1864, shall be fixed at the rate of 1,000 francs per year per man.

ARTICLE 11. The Mexican government shall at once remit to the French government the sum of 66,000,000 francs in loan securities at par, i.e., 54,000,000 to be deducted from

the debt mentioned in Article 9, and 12,000,000 as an install-
ment on the indemnities due the French under Article 14 of
the present agreement.

ARTICLE 12. In payment of the balance of war expenses
and of the charges mentioned in Articles 7, 10 and 14, the
Mexican government agrees to pay to France the annual sum
of 25,000,000 francs in cash. That said sum shall be credited,
first, to the sums due under Articles 7 and 10; second, to the
amount, interest and principal of the sum fixed in Article 9;
third, to the indemnities still due to French subjects under
Article 14 and following.

ARTICLE 13. The Mexican government shall pay on the
last day of every month, in Mexico, into the hands of the pay-
master-general of the army, the amount necessary to cover
the expense of the French troops remaining in Mexico, in
conformity with Article 10.

ARTICLE 14. The Mexican government agrees to indemnify
French subjects for the grievances unduly suffered by them
and which caused the expedition.

ARTICLE 15. A mixed commission composed of three
Frenchmen and three Mexicans, appointed by their respective governments, shall meet in Mexico within three months
to examine into and settle these claims.

ARTICLE 16. A mission of revision composed of three
Frenchmen and two Mexicans, appointed as above and sitting
in Paris, shall proceed to the definite settlement of the claims
already admitted by the commission mentioned in the preceding article, and shall pass upon those the settlement of
which shall be reserved to them.

ARTICLE 17. The French government shall set free all
Mexican prisoners of war as soon as H. M. the Emperor of
Mexico shall have entered into his Empire.

ARTICLE 18. The present convention shall be ratified and
the ratification shall be exchanged as soon as possible.

Done at the castle of Miramar, on April 10th, 1864.

HERBET.

VELÁZQUEZ.

ADDITIONAL SECRET ARTICLES

Article 1. H. M. the Emperor of Mexico, approving the principles and promises announced in General Forey's proclamation, dated June 12, 1863, as well as the measures taken by the Regency and by the French general-in-chief, in accordance with said declaration, has resolved to inform his people, by a manifesto, of his intentions in the matter.

Article 2. On his side, the Emperor of the French declares that the actual effective force of the French corps of 38,000 men shall only be reduced gradually and from year to year, in such a way that the French troops remaining in Mexico, including the foreign legion, shall be 28,000 men in 1865, 25,000 in 1866, 20,000 in 1867.

Article 3. When the said foreign legion, under the terms of Article 3 of the above convention, shall pass into the service and pay of Mexico, as it nevertheless shall continue to serve a cause in which France is interested, its generals and officers shall preserve their quality of Frenchmen and their claim to promotion in the French army according to law.

Done at the castle of Miramar, April 10, 1864.

HERBET.

VELÁZQUEZ.

APPENDICES · II

Plans for Maximilian's Escape

BEFORE the Princess Salm-Salm reached Querétaro her husband and one or two others had laid some abortive plans for aiding Maximilian to escape, but nothing had come of these, save the profitless expenditure of a few hundred pesos, the realization that the men they were working with were useless, and the creation of suspicions in the mind of Escobedo. When the Princess came on the ground, with characteristic energy and enterprise she took matters into her own hands. What followed she describes in that portion of her *Diary* which she devotes to her Mexican experiences, as follows:

"Long before this I had impressed upon him [Maximilian] the necessity of negotiating about an escape, not with inferior officers but with those highest in command. One of them I had won already; he had the command over all the guards in the city; but Colonel Palacios had also to be won, as he had command over the prison itself. For this purpose I wanted one hundred thousand dollars in gold from the Emperor, which were to be placed in the bank of Señor Rubio, to be drawn according to circumstances, for ready cash. This, I said, was the most essential thing in dealing with all Mexicans.

"The Emperor said that money was the least trouble in the affair, for Baron von Magnus [the Prussian minister] and the other ministers had assured him that money would be at his disposal to any amount. Strange! At the tail of each word of these gentlemen hung a gold ounce, but not a miserable dollar at the tip of their fingers! It is indeed excusable if I get impatient and indignant, for this paltry stinginess killed the Emperor.

"Baron von Magnus had unfortunately gone to San Luis Potosí. . . . I told the Emperor that without money I could do nothing, and he sent for Baron Lago, the Austrian chargé, who had not ventured near him for two days. I believe the great Baron belonged to that great tribe they call in Germany 'harefoots'—'*Hasenfüsse*.' He had been of the opinion that the Emperor would not be shot, and treated my apprehensions also as the fancies of a frightened woman; but of late he had become rather nervous, and was afraid these republican rascals would not only shoot the Emperor, but even the most sacred representative of his Imperial brother of Austria.

"The Emperor was indeed very much forsaken, and felt so; and when I told him that the imprisoned Imperial colonels were all to be sent away, and my husband with them, and that I should have to follow them, he was very much excited and said: 'You are the only person who has really done anything for me. If you go, I am utterly forsaken.' In consequence of this it was arranged between my husband and myself that he should now show his commission as a general, which he had not done before, as it was said that all the generals were to be shot. He was, of course, in no hurry for that. . . . My husband had written a letter to the Emperor, which I transmitted to him, in which he implored him to lose no time by resigning himself to delusive hopes, but to prepare immediately for escape, for which the plan was also contained in the letter.

"I now told the Emperor that I had arranged everything with Colonel Villanueva, who would lead him outside the prison, where a guard of one hundred men would be kept ready to escort him to the Sierra Gorda, and from thence to the coast. The Emperor insisted upon my following him closely on horseback with Dr. Basch. He was afraid of being betrayed and assassinated, and thought that the presence of a woman might be a kind of protection against such an atrocious act.

"Villanueva had, however, declared to me that nothing could be done without Palacios, who had always three guards in the prison who walked all night before the room of the

Emperor. I told the Emperor so, and that I had engaged myself to win him over, but that I required money for that purpose.

"The Emperor now saw at last his position in its true light, and regretted that he had squandered so much precious time. Unfortunately, he had no money, but he said that he would look to that and have at least five thousand dollars in gold, which I required either to give to Palacios to distribute amongst the soldiers, or to give it myself into their hands.

"When I returned again to see the Emperor he was in despair, for he could not procure the money which was required to bribe the two colonels; but he would give two bills, each for one hundred thousand dollars, signed by himself and drawn upon the Imperial family in Vienna. The five thousand dollars, however, he could not send me until nine o'clock that evening.

"I had not yet made any attempt to bribe Palacios, and it was agreed between myself and Villanueva that I should leave the prison at eight o'clock and request Palacios to see me home, where I would detain him until ten o'clock. I did not then live in the hotel, but in a private house belonging to Señora Pepita Vicente, the widow of a gentleman of our party who had died during the siege. . . . In the afternoon I had a long conversation with the Emperor. . . . When it was nearly eight o'clock the Emperor gave me his signet ring. If I succeeded with Palacios I was to return it as a token. Then I left with a very heavy heart, and filled with anxiety, for I had before me a task of the highest importance, which I had to accomplish with very insufficient means—two bits of paper, of which the meaning was scarcely known to the persons with whom I had to deal.

"Colonel Palacios was an Indian without education, who could scarcely read, or write. He was a brave soldier, had distinguished himself and won the confidence of his superiors, who employed him as a kind of provost-marshal, who had to supervise military executions. He had a young wife, who had just given him his first child, in whom the father was entirely wrapped up; and as he was poor, I hoped that his care for the future of that child might induce him to entertain my proposition.

"The Colonel escorted me home. I invited him to the *sala*. He followed, and I began to speak of the Emperor in order to ascertain how he felt in reference to him, and whether I had any chance of success. He said that he had been a great enemy of the Emperor, but after having been so long about him and having witnessed how good and noble he behaved in his misfortune, and looked into his true, melancholy eyes, he felt the greatest sympathy, if not love and admiration, for him.

"After this introductory conversation, which lasted about twenty minutes, with a trembling heart I came to the point. It was a most thrilling moment, on which indeed hung the life, or death of a noble and good man who was my friend and Emperor. I said that I had to communicate to him something which was of the greatest importance to both of us, but before doing so I must ask him whether he would give me his word of honor as an officer and a gentleman, and swear by the head of his wife and child not to divulge to anyone what I was about to confide in him, even if he rejected my proposition. He gave me his word of honor, and most solemnly swore, as I desired, by the life of his wife and child, whom he loved beyond anything else in this world.

"After that I told him I knew for certain that the Emperor could be condemned to be shot, and that he would be shot if he did not escape. I had arranged this escape through others and it would take place this very night if he would only consent to turn his back and close his eyes for ten minutes. Without this nothing could be done; we were entirely in his hands, and upon him now depended the life of the Emperor. Urged by the necessity of the situation I must speak plainly to him. I knew he was a poor man. He had a wife and a child and their future was uncertain. Now an opportunity was offered to secure them a good competency. I offered him here a check of the Emperor's for one hundred thousand dollars which would be paid by the Imperial family in Austria, and five thousand dollars which I should receive directly for the soldiers. What I proposed to him was nothing against his honor, as in accepting it he best served his country. The death of the Emperor would bring all the world in arms against it, but if the Emperor escaped he would leave the country and no European power would ever meddle with the arrangement of Mexican affairs. I spoke a good deal more, to which he listened attentively, and I saw by the changes in his countenance that he was battling hard within himself.

"At last he spoke. He laid his hand on his heart, and protested that he felt indeed the greatest sympathy with Maximilian; that he really believed it to be best for Mexico to let him escape, but he could not decide about such an important step in five minutes. If he did, he could not accept the check. He took it, however, in his hand and looked at it with curiosity. The Indian probably could not conceive the idea that in such a little rag of paper, with some scrawls on it, should be contained a life of plenty for his wife and child. A bag full of gold would have been more persuasive.

"He handed me back the check, observing that he could not accept it now. He would reflect upon it during the night, and tell me his decision the next morning. I showed him the signet ring of the Emperor, told him what it meant and requested him to accept it and return it to the Emperor that night. He took it and put it on his finger, but after a while he took it off again, remarking he could not accept it. He must think it all over. He became confused and went on speaking of his honor, his wife and his child.

" 'Well, Colonel,' said I, 'you are not well disposed. Reflect upon it, and remember your word of honor and your oath. You know that without you nothing can be done, and to betray me would serve no purpose whatever.'

"Colonel Villanueva came to see how matters went, but

without betraying that he was in the secret. Directly after him came Dr. Basch, sent by the Emperor, but without any money. Palacios left me about ten o'clock, not knowing whether I might hope, or not, but rather inclined to hope. I told Dr. Basch I believed all would be right, but that I should not know for certain before morning.

"In reference to the two checks which the Emperor gave me I mention a circumstance illustrating the character of the Austrian chargé, Baron Lago. The Emperor had desired that the two papers might be signed by the foreign ministers, especially by the representative of Austria, who had been so free with their promises of money. Dr. Basch was entrusted with that commission. When he entered the room and told his errand, Lago, forgetting all his diplomatic dignity, jumped about the room like a rabbit, tore his hair and cried piteously: 'We cannot sign them! If we do we shall all be hanged!' The other ministers present, although less undignified, also remonstrated, and Lago, whose signature was already under the checks, for he had signed in the presence of the Emperor, took courage by the cowardice of his fellow representatives, and resolutely taking a pair of scissors, he cut off his signature!

"When Dr. Basch returned with the mutilated checks to his master and mentioned the fear of the Baron being hanged, the Emperor said: 'What would it matter? The world would not lose much.'

"Returning from my house after my conversation with Palacios, Dr. Basch told the Emperor what he had heard from me of the conversation. Maximilian seemed to fear that I would be swindled out of the checks, which might be presented for payment after he was shot. He therefore ordered the Doctor to bring me next morning the following paper, written by his own hand, in Spanish:

Querétaro, 13 of June, 1867,

The two bills of one hundred thousand dollars each which I signed today for the Colonels Palacios and Villanueva, to be paid by the house and the Imperial family of Austria in Vienna, are only valid on the day when I regain my complete liberty through the efforts of the above mentioned Colonels.

MAXIMILIAN.

"Colonel Palacios seems to have reflected on my propositions until midnight. Then he made up his mind and accordingly went to Escobedo and divulged to him the whole affair. Escobedo sent me away from Querétaro the next morning. I never saw the Emperor again."

Disposition of Maximilian's Body

THE reasons that moved Juárez to refuse to release his hold on Maximilian's body and permit it to be taken care of by his friends can only be conjectured. Without mentioning details of too unpleasant a nature, the evidence is that the body was handled with a notable lack of elementary respect, or even decency. Frederick Hall, an American lawyer, who acted as legal adviser to Maximilian in Querétaro until he was sent away from the city by Escobedo, writes:

"The physicians had no naphtha to use in the work [of embalming] but injected chloride of zinc into the arteries and veins, having taken out the intestines, heart, liver, lungs, etc., leaving the frame by itself. That operation lasted three days. During these nights the body was kept in alcohol, save the head. It was varnished twice, each time occupying two days in drying, and was hung up for that purpose. Nearly eight days were occupied in completing the process of embalming.

"All the parts taken from the body were prepared by being mixed with the powder of tannin and galls. The body was afterwards dressed in black trousers, military boots, with the blue campaign coat which the deceased wore, with plain gilt buttons buttoned up to the neck; black neck-tie and black kid gloves. Black glass eyes were placed over his natural ones. Glass eyes of the color of Maximilian's could not be obtained. Robbing the face of a portion of its beard and the head of its hair, and changing the color of the eyes, had somewhat disfigured the remains.

"The coffin in which the body was placed was made of cedar and lined with zinc. Within the metallic lining was another of cambric. Under the head was placed a black velvet pillow trimmed with gold thread, with gilt tassels at the four corners. The exterior of the coffin was covered with black velvet, ornamented with bands of gold lace. The cover over the face was of glass. Near the foot of the coffin and parallel with it were two small compartments, one on each side and about two feet in length. In the one on the left hand were deposited the heart, liver and lungs; and in the other the remainder of the substances taken from the body all of which were mixed with charcoal and chloride of lime.

"The coffin thus arranged, with its contents, was placed in one of the churches at Querétaro and subsequently removed to the governor's quarters. For the first two or three weeks after embalming, the body looked tolerably well, but a month's time darkened it, and it soon gave increasing evidence that the work of preservation had been badly done. While in the quarters of the governor it was seen with the glass cover cracked and spotted with candle-grease, as though stowed away like so much worthless trash.

"Not many days had elapsed after the termination of the foregoing correspondence [notes relative to the disposition of the body exchanged between the Mexican foreign minister and representatives of the Austrian government] when it was transported to the city of Mexico and deposited in the hospital of San Andrés. It was soon observed that decay was working so rapidly upon it that it became necessary to make some preparations to arrest its progress. When the cloth bandages were taken off for that purpose, the odor of putrefaction was very noticeable. It was bathed for some time in a solution of arsenic, which assisted in its preservation for a short while; but it was apparent that it would not long be recognizable. The face was much sunken in and the whole features were gradually changing. . . . After the second process of attempted preservation of the body was completed, it was attired in a suit of black and laid in a new coffin made of a granadilla wood, which was elegantly polished and ornamented with a few carvings."

In connection with the temporary depositing of Maximilian's

body in the hospital of San Andrés a curious incident developed which is told by Don José María Marroqui in his *Streets of Mexico:*

"To the chapel attached to the hospital of San Andrés was brought the body of Emperor Maximilian, which had been hastily embalmed at Querétaro. Orders were issued that the corpse be treated in a manner which would permit of it being transported to Austria. The task was entrusted to a commission of medical men, consisting of Dr. Agustín Andrade, Dr. Rafael Montaño and Dr. Felipe Buenrostro. In Querétaro the embalming had been hastily done by injecting preservative fluids in the veins and arteries. This was not considered efficacious by the physicians named. In fact, the corpse was already exhibiting signs of decomposition. Accordingly the physicians adopted a method of desiccation, similar to that employed by the ancient Egyptians. The fluids of the body were drained off until it was sufficiently dry to enable it to be wrapped in bandages and varnished. In order to do this more easily, and also to facilitate the replacing of the dead Emperor's garments, it was necessary to suspend it from the ceiling by ropes for several days. According to the notes made by Dr. Andrade the body was under treatment from September 13 until November 4. The actual work occupied 70 hours, the remainder of the time being required for the drying of the varnish used in the process.

"I mention these facts so minutely," Marroqui explains, "because of the influence exerted by them upon subsequent events.

"On the first anniversary of the Emperor's death, June 19, 1868, the adherents of Maximilian and the Empire held a memorial service in the chapel of St. Andrés, at which the sermon was preached by Father Mario Cavalieri, an Italian Jesuit. The chapel was chosen for the ceremony because of the Emperor's body having rested there. The intemperate language indulged in by Father Cavalieri, who did not content himself with eulogizing the dead Emperor, but launched into violent attacks upon Juárez and his government, led Juárez to order that the chapel be demolished. This work was begun without warning on the night of July 28. Not only was the chapel torn down, but also a part of the hospital at its rear, to permit the cutting through of a new street.

"While according to common report the government was led to decide upon the demolition of the chapel because of the sermon preached there by Father Cavalieri, this was merely the drop of water which caused the glass to overflow. From the time the Emperor's body had lain in the chapel, the place became a center for those who had supported the Empire and for opponents of the government generally. Seizing on the fact that the Emperor's corpse had been suspended while it was undergoing the second embalming process, the Imperialists made of this incident a political epigram, which ran to the effect that although the 'Puros,' as the Liberals were called, had sought to catch Maximilian while he was alive and hang him, they had succeeded in this only after he was dead. The chapel became known as 'The Chapel of the Martyr,' and was converted into a focus whence the Imperialists radiated discontent and disapproval of the Liberals and of the Juárez government.

"This was the state of affairs when the memorial service was held. Father Cavalieri had the Italian faculty for perfervid oratory. His sermon on this occasion moved his orators to intensely emotional reactions. When he had finished, they poured into the street, sobbing, denouncing the government and Juárez, and raising such a tumult that the police were required to prevent rioting.

"When the governor of the Federal District, Don Juan José Baz, reported to President Juárez what had happened, Juárez said to him dryly:

" 'Do you not know a man of the name of Baz who will pull down this chapel for me?'

" 'Yes, I know him,' replied Baz, 'I will tell him and he will pull it down.'

"Given his authority in this semi-humorous fashion, Baz, who manifestly was a man of action, laid his plans for the destruction of the chapel. Both he and Juárez appreciated that unless the job was done promptly, and if their intentions became known, troublesome opposition probably would arise. It was therefore desirable, in order to avert hostile demonstrations from the Imperialists and the clericals, while the work was in progress, that extraordinary and rapid measures be taken. Baz quietly summoned all the Liberal architects he had heard of who had had experience in similar church-wrecking enterprises, but none of them would promise to level the chapel as speedily as Baz demanded.

"Baz then took the matter into his own hands and arranged to attack the solidly constructed building after an ingenious fashion of his own. He first got together hundreds of wedges, fashioned of the same kind of wood, all equal in size and thoroughly dry. Without warning he appeared at the gate of the hospital, of which the chapel was a part, late on the night of June 28, nine days after the delivery of the offensive sermon by Father Cavalieri. With him were a number of men bearing stretchers, of the sort used in carrying sick, or wounded persons. On the stretchers were the wedges, and behind the governor was a throng of masons, armed with crowbars, chisels, mallets, hammers and other implements of their craft.

"Once inside, the governor set his men at work upon the dome of the chapel. He disposed them in such manner that as many as possible might apply themselves effectively without interfering with the movements of their fellows. The object of the masons was to make a circular cut about the base of the dome, close to the roof, by removing the masonry and inserting wedges in the vacant places. Within a few hours the dome was wholly detached from the surrounding masonry and rested entirely upon the wedges. Before being inserted the wedges had been well soaked in turpentine. When everything was ready, fresh turpentine was applied to the wedges, all of which were ignited simultaneously.

"As the wedges were reduced to ashes the dome settled and finally just at daybreak crashed to the floor of the church with a resounding roar and in a cloud of dust. Fresh relays of workmen came and kept up operations on the chapel day and night until it was leveled to its foundations. To prevent the rebuilding of the chapel upon any pretext, or the leaving of a chance that the ground upon which it had stood might again be employed for religious purposes, or as a gathering place for disaffected political elements, the government opened a street through the site."

Notes

Notes

1. Sara Yorke Stevenson, who was a witness of events in Mexico in 1864–67, in her *Maximilian in Mexico,* supplies an excellent pen portrait of the personalities of the Emperor and the Empress. The scene is a court ball at which the author was present: "Maximilian was happy in his remarks on such occasions. Naturally affable and kindly, his memory for faces and names was remarkable. . . . He was tall, slight and handsome, although the whole expression of his face denoted weakness and indecision. He looked, and was, a gentleman. His dignity was without hauteur. His manner was attractive; he had the faculty of making one feel at ease, and he possessed far more personal magnetism than Carlota. Hers was a strong, intelligent face, the lines of which were somewhat hard at times, and her determined expression impressed one with the feeling that she was the better equipped of the two to cope intelligently with the difficulties of practical life. . . . She, however, was reserved, somewhat lacking in tact and adaptability; and a certain haughtiness of manner, a dignity too conscious of itself, at first repelled any who were disposed to feel kindly toward her." When they came to Mexico Maximilian was 32 and Carlota 24. Carlota did not die until 1926.

2. Of Eloin Mrs. Stevenson says: "He was an obscure personal favorite who had risen to favor through his social accomplishments. This man did not speak a word of Spanish, hated the French, despised the Mexicans and was more ignorant than his master of American questions in general and of Mexican affairs in particular. His narrow views were responsible for a jealous policy which excluded all that he could not personally appreciate and manage. . . . After doing much mischief Eloin was sent abroad upon a mysterious mission. It was rumored that he had to watch over his master's interests abroad."

This mission probably had to do with the fact that on December 28, 1864, Maximilian entered a protest against the family compact exacted from him by Franz Joseph on April 9, a few days before Maximilian left Miramar for Mexico, and which had been communicated to the Austrian Reichrath on November 16. In the protest Maximilian stated: that the throne of Mexico had been offered him at the suggestion of Franz Joseph; that after he had accepted it, and his withdrawal would have brought about European complications, the Emperor, with some of his councillors, had come in haste to Miramar to compel him to renounce absolutely his rights to the Austrian throne, etc.; that he had signed the renunciation because he had solemnly promised to go to Mexico; that jurists and diplomats were of the opinion that a document signed under such conditions was null and void; and that only the Diets of Austria, with the consent of Franz Joseph and Maximilian, were competent to decide on the question of Maximilian's rights. A few months later, Eloin left Mexico on his mission. This concerned Maximilian's dynastic rights, as is clearly indicated by the letter from Eloin to Maximilian, dated September 17, 1866, which was intercepted by Juárez. (See this volume, p. 119.)

3. Some of these articles, including parts of silver-plated ware, remain in the National Museum; and other fittings are still in the palace and at Chapultepec.

4. Originally there were three floors in the palace: ground, mezzanine and first; the present third floor was added in recent years.

5. The coach was presented to Maximilian by the citizens of Milan, when he was Governor of Venice-Lombardy.

6. General Juan N. Almonte was an illegitimate son of Morelos, the militant priest who continued the rebellion against the Spaniards after the death of Hidalgo who headed the first revolt in Mexico in 1810. Almonte seems to have been a man of courage and of measurable honesty and steadfastness of loyalty and purpose. Although by his diligence and skill in presenting the cause of the clericals and the Conservatives in Europe he had contributed, probably more than any other person, to the establishment of the Empire, Maximilian rewarded him only with empty, high-sounding honors, and positions about the court. But it was Almonte whom he chose to go to Paris to endeavor to induce Napoleon to continue financial and military support to the Empire.

7. Bazaine was described by Mrs. Stevenson, who knew him, as: ". . . a plain looking man, short and thickest, whose plebeian features one might search in vain for a spark of genius or a ray of imagination; and yet, under the commonplace exterior, dwelt a

kindly spirit, and intelligence of no mean order." Bazaine's first wife died in France, while he was in Mexico.

8. The palace is now used as a cigarette factory. It was given, or sold, by Juárez to Rincon Gallardo, the Liberal officer who permitted Maximilian temporarily to escape when Querétaro was captured by the Liberals in 1867.

9. Stevenson describes Forey as: ". . . a very heavy man, of full habit, with a short neck and a red complexion, all the more ruddy by contrast with his gray hair and mustache. He was most unpopular. . . . General Forey's elevation had been due mainly to the fact that he was one of the men who had served Napoleon in 1851 in the *coup d'état.*"

10. Agustín Iturbide, grandson of Emperor Iturbide, died in March, 1925, in Washington, D.C., where he had lived for many years.

11. Niox, in *L'Expédition du Mexique,* quotes Carlota as writing in a private letter: "The Austrians and the Belgians are very good when everything is quiet, but in time of trouble we can count only on the red trousers (the French)."

12. Miramón is described by Stevenson: "Miramón was barely twenty-six when he arose to first rank in Mexican politics. Of Béarnese extraction, his father's family having passed over to Spain in the eighteenth century, his grandfather had gone to Mexico as aide-de-camp to one of the viceroys. Miguel Miramón had served in the war against the United States. He was a brilliant officer, bold, daring, vigorous and original. During his term as president he had on his side the clergy, the army, the capital."

13. Márquez shot a number of civilians, including physicians who had cared for the wounded after a battle in the plaza of Tacubaya, a suburb of Mexico City. This earned for him the title, "The Tiger of Tacubaya."

14. Langlais had charge of virtually the entire fiscal system of the Empire and oversaw other important branches of the government.

15. As early as 1865 the chief buttress of the Empire in France disappeared, with the death of the Duc de Morny, Napoleon's illegitimate brother, of whom Stevenson says: "On March 10th, 1865, the Duc de Morny died. He had been the moving spirit in the Mexican embroglio and it would be difficult to believe that the withdrawal of the prompter did not have a weakening effect upon

the performance. His death, by removing one of the strongest influences in favor of the intervention, not only in the Corps Législative and at court, but also in the financial world, was certainly one of the untoward circumstances which helped to hasten the end."

16. Gaulot, in *L'Empire de Maximilien,* quotes Bazaine as writing to the French Minister of War: "The Emperor Maximilian, whose character appears to be essentially patient, wanted to wait until Juárez had left Mexican territory before promulgating the law. His Majesty finally decided, *upon my advice,* to give a proof of firmness which would have a good effect upon the Conservatives."

17. Benito Pablo Juárez was of pure Indian extraction, and began life as a servant in a wealthy family of Oaxaca, his native state. His talents led his employer to give him an education. He soon rose to eminence as a lawyer, became a member of national congresses, state governor and finally president. He died suddenly in the National Palace, in 1872.

18. Stevenson says: "General Riva Palacios was a patriot and a gentleman . . . [with] some reputation as a poet and a dramatic author. At the outbreak of the war he organized and equipped a regiment at his own expense and was with General Zaragoza at Puebla [at the defeat of the first effort of the French army to capture that city]. His division was one of the finest in the Mexican service and . . . he conducted his campaigns in strict accordance with recognized usages. He cared for the wounded, exchanged prisoners and, at the last, even went to the length of extending his protection to small detachments of French troops making their way to the Gulf coast from the shores of the Pacific."

19. A great many more or less sensational and apocryphal accounts have been written upon what took place between Napoleon and Carlota. Eugénie, in her memoirs, probably stated the facts with reasonable accuracy:

"Empress Charlotte had just reached Paris and without taking any rest asked an audience of Napoleon. Immediately an Imperial carriage was sent to the hotel . . . and the Empress was brought to the Palace [St. Cloud] on August 11, at 2 o'clock in the afternoon. The guard then on duty showed her royal honors. She was in an open victoria and bowed graciously, I remember, as she passed the national flag at the gate. The carriage stopped in front of the vestibule leading to our private apartments, where stood the Emperor and the Empress ready to meet the guest, and together they mounted the staircase. . . . The Empress Charlotte was then only twenty-six years of age, tall, imposing and elegant, with an oval face which bore marks of great anxiety; fine, large brown eyes and graceful features in every respect. She wore a long, black silk dress, an elegant white hat, and was every inch a queen, physically, intellectually and in outward appearance.

"A little later, for two hours the unhappy princess, with all the resolution and eloquence born of great misfortunes, told the pitiful tale of trials and difficulties of all sorts against which Maximilian had struggled, a prey to the revolutionary agitations of the country, to open treason and to every possible opposition on the part of ambitious politicians, both native and foreign. . . . It was absolutely necessary that the Emperor refuse any further support to Maximilian, or to interfere again in Mexican affairs. He repeated, therefore, that he could give no help, and, moreover, after trying to open the eyes of the Empress Charlotte to the real situation, he urged her at all hazards to induce her husband to give up such a desperate enterprise, such a forlorn hope, and sail back to Europe. Such a response was not at all what the Princess had expected, for she was blinded by illusions. . . . She suggested all sorts of plans. One of these was to go even to Rome and beg the help of the Holy Father; another, to make a supreme effort with the Emperor of Austria and a third, to urge the King of the Belgians to come to their aid. When the poor Empress left, her weary face and fatigued features generally told of the tears she had forced back. . . . When this distressing interview was ended, Empress Charlotte walked unassisted to her carriage, apparently seeing nothing. She declined the hand of the aide-de-camp who wished to help her to the seat and then, falling back upon the cushions in a despairing attitude, she even forgot, in her sorrow, to salute the flag which bent over her from the castle wall."

20. Briefly, these had been the developments in Mexico after Blasio started for Europe and before his return: Both in a political and military way the affairs of the Empire had declined, swiftly and alarmingly. Carlota's failure with Napoleon and the Pope was followed by news of her illness. In October the Emperor left the capital for Orizaba. There is little doubt that he had then fully determined to abdicate and go to Europe. By that time Father

Fischer had become Maximilian's chief adviser and the head of his personal cabinet. The impending abandonment of Mexico and the throne by Maximilian threw the Imperialists into consternation. They realized that their only hope of personal and political salvation was rooted in maintaining the Empire, with Maximilian, temporarily, at least, at its head. The alarm of the church party at the impending triumph of Juárez and the Liberals made them hasten to employ their influence upon Maximilian, through Fischer, to cajole him into remaining in Mexico. Fischer accompanied him to Orizaba. From then until Blasio's return the Imperialists and the clericals worked unceasingly upon Maximilian and, in the end, as Blasio tells, successfully. Early in October General Castelnau, the personal aide-de-camp of Napoleon, arrived in Vera Cruz, entrusted with the mission of endeavoring to devise a workable plan whereby Maximilian might be induced to abdicate and his government succeeded by other, and purely Mexican, machinery which would control the country. Although Maximilian and Castelnau passed each other a few miles from the City of Mexico, the Emperor refused then to see him. They did not meet until several weeks later at Puebla, after Maximilian had committed himself to remaining on the throne.

21. "Father Fischer was an obscure adventurer of low degree," says Stevenson, "and of more than shady reputation, whose shrewdness and talent for intrigue had impressed themselves upon the weakened mind of the Emperor in the latter days of his reign. Utterly unscrupulous, with everything to gain for himself and his party, with absolutely nothing to lose but a life which he took good care to save by avoiding danger, he insinuated himself into the confidence of Maximilian and became the Mephistopheles of the last act of the Mexican drama."

After Maximilian's death Fischer remained in Mexico and spent his last days in charge of San Cosme parish in the capital. It is said that Fischer was offered $30,000 by the French to induce Maximilian to abdicate.

22. According to Stevenson, the new army that Maximilian hoped to create was to have been formed about the Mexican Chasseurs, an effective force of 15,000 men, to which it was planned to add ten regiments of cavalry. The first of these was commanded by Colonel Miguel López, the traitor. In December, 1866, three companies of gendarmes, in all about 1,200 men, were organized

under the Belgian, Colonel Tigdal. A regiment of Red Hussars, composed of the remnants of the disbanded Austrians, about 700 men, was placed in command of Colonel von Kevenhüller, and this, with the Austrian regiment of Colonel Hammerstein, finally completed the new organization, with what few thousand scattered Mexican forces there were about the country that were still loyal. Hammerstein was killed in the trenches in May, 1867, when the capital was being besieged by the Liberals under General Porfirio Díaz. A large number of French, the best of whom had been detached from their national military service with the official sanction of their government, had entered the imperial army and received from the Mexican government their equipment and a bounty. They had formed the framework and the backbone of the new regiments, for the clothing and arming of which Maximilian had strained every nerve, going so far as to sacrifice his silver plate.

23. In the belief that Maximilian's abdication was only a matter of weeks and desiring to exercise its good offices in enabling Juárez and the Liberals to set up a stable government in succession to the Empire, the United States government sent General William T. Sherman and three other commissioners to confer with Juárez, or his representatives. They reached Vera Cruz the day Maximilian's proclamation was issued, and promptly returned to the United States without attempting then or later to comply with their mission.

24. A strong feeling existed among the French officials in Mexico, says Stevenson, against Dano, who was openly accused by them of pursuing a policy dictated by personal interest. He had married a Mexican whose dowry was derived from interests in the Real del Monte mines near Pachuca, and the Imperialists suspected that the weight of Dano's influence was thrown on the side of the Liberals with the object of safeguarding his wife's wealth. Stevenson says: "When General Castelnau arrived Maximilian was hesitating. The presence of Napoleon's aide-de-camp was not calculated to soothe his feelings. The return of Generals Márquez and Miramón at this crisis again turned the tide of events. These men, formerly set aside from French influence, felt a resentment which added strength to their party feeling. The confidence of the Emperor in their ability once more to rally the people about his banner, through the influence of the clergy, triumphed over his in-

decision. Señor Lares had promised him the immediate control of four million dollars [pesos?] and of an army ready to take the field. Now here were old, experienced leaders to take command. He hesitated no longer. Breaking with all declared principles of policy, he threw himself into the arms of the clerical party, and pledging himself to reinstate the clergy and to return to the church its confiscated property, he prepared to play his last hand without the French."

25. General Porfirio Díaz once told the editor that Bazaine had offered to sell him a quantity of French war supplies on the eve of the latter's withdrawal from Mexico, and that he had refused to buy them.

26. Concerning the Salm-Salms the following was written by Stevenson: "Prince Salm-Salm and his handsome American wife came to Mexico in 1866. They found serious difficulty in gaining admittance into either the social, or the official circles of the capital. . . . A Prussian subject, the Prince was naturally looked upon with distrust by the Austrians. He had brought letters from Baron Yerold, the Prussian minister at Washington; from Baron von Wydenbruck, the Austrian minister, and from Marquis de Montholon, the French minister, but these seemed unable to win for him even a hearing from the Emperor. . . . When, six months after his arrival in Mexico the most unremitting efforts on his part at last obtained for him a commission, and he was given the rank of Colonel in the auxiliary corps under General Neigre, he was treated with no especial cordiality. From this time he and his attractive wife obscurely followed the fortunes of Colonel Van der Smissen, whose personal regard they had won, until the withdrawal of the French and the Austro-Belgian armies, by clearing the stage for the last scene, brought them into full relief, under the searchlight of history, by the side of the Imperial victim. . . . The Salm-Salms bravely stood by the Emperor to the bitter end, when older and more valued, though less courageous, friends had dropped away and left him, stripped of the Imperial purple, to struggle for existence, an adventurer among adventurers."

27. Before he died Maximilian knew that Márquez had coldly and deliberately deserted him. Once in the capital, Márquez set himself up as a dictator, misusing the authority given him by the Emperor, raised heavy forced loans, collected as many troops as he could and marched to the east of the city to give battle to the

Liberals under General Porfirio Díaz. Díaz routed him at San Lorenzo. "Márquez fled," says Stevenson, "with 200 cavalry, leaving his beaten army, then pursued by 16,000 men, to extricate itself as best it might. Colonel Kodolitch then assumed command and fighting his way through the enemy brought back the débris of the Imperial force, now reduced to one-third, to the capital, where Márquez had preceded him."

When Díaz later on besieged the City of Mexico, the European military men were so disgusted with the cowardice of Márquez that they only nominally recognized his leadership and considered themselves under the command of Kodolich. By concealing himself in an unoccupied grave in one of the cemeteries, Márquez saved his life when the Liberals entered the city, and eventually escaped to Cuba, where he remained for twenty-seven years before venturing to return to Mexico. Márquez, who earned his nickname, "The Tiger of Tacubaya," because of the atrocious and summary death inflicted by his orders upon several young Mexican physicians and medical students who were caring for the wounded after one of the battles under the presidency of Miramón, was one of those sinister and temporarily glittering figures that abound in Mexican history.

28. The *New York Herald* of July 2, 1867, says: "The fate of the officer who betrayed Querétaro and the Emperor is doubtful. He was seen in Querétaro at large the day after the surrender. That he had received then his promised reward seems unlikely, since he made application to one of the leading Liberal officers for relief. Meeting Colonel Rincon Gallardo he said: 'Colonel, I am not, like you, a rich man with many haciendas. I have nothing but my sword to depend upon. I hope you will recommend me for a position in the Liberal army.' Rincon [the same man who tried to let Maximilian escape] is reported to have replied: 'Colonel López, if I recommend you to any position, it will be to a position on a tree with a rope around your neck.' " López' treason seems to have been adequately established, regardless of his own defence and that made by others.

"Colonel López," says Stevenson, "was highly thought of by the French, who had conferred upon him the red ribbon of the Legion of Honor. He was appointed to act on the Imperial escort when the monarch landed at Vera Cruz, and made himself agreeable to him. The dragoons of the Empress, of which he was commander, were regarded as one of the best regiments in the army. The man's political and military past, however, did not bear investigation, and when Maximilian, whose favorite he had become, thought of promoting him to the rank of general, the best among the Mexican officers in the Imperial army requested General Méndez to inform the Emperor of his record. It has been stated that his disappointed hopes influenced his conduct in the dark transactions through which his name has been handed down to lasting infamy."

López sought to exculpate himself, after Maximilian's death, by trying to prove that the Emperor had ordered him to treat with the Liberals for the delivery of Querétaro into their hands, with the understanding that they would spare Maximilian's life. The document bearing the alleged signature of Maximilian which López produced in support of this story was revealed to be a forgery. Blasio is not alone in recording the admission of Liberal officers that López betrayed Maximilian. Had he not done so, it is reasonable to assume that the Liberals would not have been backward in claiming for their arms full and exclusive credit for the taking of the city.

29. Stevenson: "It was General Méndez who in October, 1865, had carried out the provisions of the proclamation of Maximilian, condemning to summary execution enemies of the Empire who were taken with arms in hand, by shooting Generals Arteaga and Salazar. He could therefore expect no mercy from the Liberals. He was condemned at once and, as a traitor, was shot with his back to four soldiers who carried out the sentence. Struck with four bullets, but not killed, Méndez arose and turning to the men begged that he be despatched. A corporal then stepped forward and blew out his brains. Méndez was a courageous soldier. Always victorious, he was beloved of his men and was highly spoken of by the French in Mexico."

30. Had Maximilian been willing to save his own life at the expense of those of Mejía and Miramón, he could probably have done so, with the assistance of the Salm-Salms. Of this episode Stevenson writes: "Three officers were bribed by Princess Salm-Salm and steps were taken to provide the necessary disguises and conveyance for the party. The plan was for them to make for the Sierra Gorda, whence the port of Tuxpan on the gulf of Mexico could be reached. From this point the party could proceed to Vera Cruz, then still holding out against the Juaristas. The Austrian frigate 'Elisabeth,' under Captain von Groeller, was at anchor in that

port, awaiting the Emperor's pleasure. The project had been seriously complicated by the positive refusal on the part of Maximilian to fly without Generals Mejía and Miramón. All details, however, were at last satisfactorily settled and the night of June 2 fixed for the attempt. On this night the officers whose goodwill had been secured were to be on guard, and the plot seemed easy of execution. But once more the innate indecision of Maximilian's character interfered. For some trivial cause he postponed the venture and thus lost his opportunity."

In her *Mexican Diary,* Princess Salm-Salm gives a circumstantial account of the attempts to rescue Maximilian. (See Appendix.) According to her, the scheme failed partly through lack of enough ready money and partly because one of the officers who had promised to accept a bribe became frightened and divulged the plot to Escobedo. She also criticizes Baron von Magnus, the Prussian minister, for refusing to guarantee the drafts which were to be given as the price of Maximilian's freedom. Her strictures upon the Austrian chargé are severe. The chargé appears to have satisfied himself, with no warrant, that his imperial master, Emperor Franz Joseph, would feel more secure on his throne if Maximilian were not alive.

31. The papers to which Maximilian referred are probably those in his private archives, which were taken from the City of Mexico to Vera Cruz and placed aboard an Austrian frigate in the latter part of 1866, when Maximilian had temporarily decided to return to Europe. They have recently become available to Count Egon Caesar Corti who utilizes them freely in his *Maximilian and Charlotte,* which was published in German in Vienna in 1924.

32. Maximilian's trial and most of the pseudo-legal machinery which was set in motion to provide an appearance of legality to the proceedings were a travesty. Juárez and Escobedo would be satisfied with nothing less than his life. Hall, an American lawyer who chanced to be in Querétaro, participated in the early stages of the preparations for Maximilian's defence, in an advisory capacity, until Escobedo ordered him to leave the city. He quotes Maximilian as saying: "When the charges were read to me I had to put my hand to my face to keep from laughing. They were so silly." In the opinion of Hall, which was shared by Mexican lawyers, the process by which Maximilian was condemned was unconstitutional and contrary to international law. The relations be-

tween the Juárez and the United States governments at that time
were of such a close nature that there is little room for doubting
that properly firm, prompt, and energetic representations from
Washington would have saved Maximilian's life, as forty-six years
later, in 1913, they would have prevented the murder of President
Madero and Vice President Pino Suárez.

33. Evidence is conflicting as to whether Maximilian believed
Carlota to be alive or dead. Probably he himself was in doubt. One
of his farewell letters was addressed to Carlota. It is reasonable to
believe that he wrote this on the chance that she might still be living. While he was in prison in Querétaro a false report, to which he
evidently gave at least partial credence, reached him that the Empress had died. In one of his last letters he directed that he be
buried by her side. His wedding ring he sent to his mother by Dr.
Basch.

34. "During the cruel weeks of mingled hope and despair that
had elapsed since he left the capital for Orizaba," says Stevenson
in commenting on Maximilian at Querétaro, "Maximilian had con-
quered self. Now the ambitious Austrian prince, the weak tool of
intriguing politicians, the upholder of religious and political retro-
gression, disappears; and where he had stood posterity will hence-
forth see only the noble son of the Hapsburgs, the well-bred gentleman who, aware of his failure, was ready to stand by it and to
pay the extreme penalty of his errors. Before the figure of Maximilian of Austria, from the time he took command of his little army
and resolved to stand for better or worse by those who had remained faithful to his fallen fortunes, all true-hearted men must
bow with respect. From that time forth his words and his acts were
noble; and in his attitude at this supreme moment, his incapacity
as a chief executive, his moral and intellectual limitations as a man,
are overlooked. We forget that he was no leader when we see how
well he could die."

35. Notwithstanding his religion, Maximilian was a Mason. He
was initiated into the fraternity and into several degrees of Scottish Rite masonry in Paris, when a very young man. In Mexico he
declined an election as grand master of the Scottish Rite body in
that country, but served in an honorary capacity as protector of
the order, and contributed generously to the funds of the organization.

36. "Who are responsible for Max's death?" the *New York*

Herald asked on July 2, 1867. "Whether some responsibility does not rest with the State Department at Washington for the muddle they have made of the Mexican legation the country will determine. Had there been a United States Minister in San Luis Potosí on the 20th (sic) of June, as there might have been, and ought to have been, Maximilian's blood would never have been shed."

This seems a reasonable opinion, and one which is apparently borne out by the facts. The Washington government, for some unknown reason, had no representative with Juárez. It was keeping in touch with him through the Mexican Minister in Washington who was himself out of direct and speedy communication with him. It is true that on April 6, 1867, the State Department had instructed one Lewis D. Campbell to proceed at once to Mexico to intercede for Maximilian. Campbell had borne the title of Minister to Mexico since May, 1866, but on various pretexts had not gone to that country. He accompanied General Sherman and other commissioners as far as Vera Cruz in the fall of 1866, but returned to New Orleans. After that Secretary Seward permitted him to continue in his office, still carefully keeping himself out of Mexico. On April 6 he was specifically instructed to "communicate to President Juárez promptly and by effectual means the desire of the United States government that in case of capture the Prince Maximilian and his supporters may receive the humane treatment accorded by civilized nations to prisoners of war." Campbell sent representations to this effect to Juárez by a messenger. No attention was paid to them, except through an evasive reply given by the Mexican Minister in Washington. Under pressure from Napoleon and the Austrian court, Secretary Seward on June 11 again telegraphed Campbell, who was at New Orleans, peremptory instructions to "proceed with as much despatch as possible to the residence of the President of Mexico and enter upon your mission. Earnestly urge clemency to Maximilian and other prisoners of war if necessary." Campbell paid no attention to them. Mr. Seward afterwards repeated the instructions. Maximilian was then under sentence of death. Campbell waited until the fifteenth and then informed Mr. Seward that he was ill and that his physician had ordered him not to travel. On the same day his resignation was asked for by Mr. Seward. Then, more or less diligently, the State Department sought to make its intervention effective, but it was too late.

37. Blasio either intentionally omits, or was not aware of, an incident connected with the execution that pathetically and eloquently illustrates the quality of superstitiousness, ingenuousness, naïveté—call it what one will—which in so many cases is found underlying the Mexican character. Mejía was a full-blooded Indian, a man of great natural ability, with high qualities of leadership, fighting skill and loyalty, but comparatively unlettered. Maximilian and the two generals the night before the execution were arranging the relative positions they would take before the firing squads, as they had been told that they were to be shot simultaneously. It was taken as a matter of course that Maximilian should stand between the generals.

"With your approval, Don Tomás, upon which I count," said the Emperor to Mejía, "we shall give Miramón the place of honor, if it is such, upon my right."

Mejía pondered for a moment before replying:

"Very well, Your Majesty, it shall be as you say, but this I am thinking: The Saviour died, they tell us, between two thieves, and they say that the one on His right was repentant, while the other was not. I am not a thief, Your Majesty, and I am not unrepentant, for I am truly sorry for whatever sins I have committed. But, if I stand on the left hand of Your Majesty, you see . . ."

"Such a *tontito* [little fool] you are, Don Tomás," said the Emperor affectionately, throwing an arm over the shoulders of the squat little Indian, "what difference does it make where we stand? We are all going the same road. Good, you shall be in the center and I shall be the unrepentant thief, for I truly believe that I am the greatest sinner of us three. I had only thought that I should like to die supported by the two most devoted of my followers, those to whom I owe most and whom I most love."

The swart, rugged features of the Indian general lighted up and he cried:

"No matter, Your Majesty, say no more. I shall stand on the left. It is an honor to die with you, to be permitted to face in your company *las cinco balas* [the five bullets; a Mexican firing squad is by custom usually composed of six men, in the weapon of one of whom a blank cartridge is placed]. Perhaps, after you, it will be permitted me to enter Heaven first, before Miramón. That will make us, him and me, even."

Stevenson's account of the execution says: "On arriving at the Cerro de las Campanas . . . the fallen Emperor looked about him for a friendly face, and finding only his servant, Tudos, the Hungarian, he asked: 'Is no one else here?' It is said, however, that Baron von Magnus, the Prussian minister, and Bahnsen, the German consul, were present, although out of sight. The good priest weakened under the ordeal, and the Emperor held his own smelling bottle to his nose. Followed by Generals Miramón and Mejía, Maximilian walked toward the open square, where an adobe wall had been erected, before which they were expected to stand. About to take his position in the middle, Maximilian stopped, and turning to General Miramón said: 'A brave soldier should be honored even in his last hour. Permit me to give you the place of honor,' and he made way for him. He then laid his hands on his breast and looked straight before him. Five shots fired at close range struck the body. He fell, and as he still moved, the officer in charge pointed to his heart with his sword and a soldier stepped forward and fired a last shot."

Dr. Basch says: "The head was free from wounds. Of the six shots received in the body, three had struck the abdomen and three the breast, almost in a straight line. The shots were fired at closest range and the six bullets so perforated the body that not a single one was found. The three wounds in the chest were mortal; one had reached the heart, the two ventricles; the second had cut the great arteries and the third had gone through the right lung. From the nature of the wounds the death struggle must have been very brief, and the words attributed to the Emperor, giving anew the word of command to fire could not have been pronounced. The motion of the hands which was observed must have been the convulsive motions which, according to physiological laws, accompany death caused by sudden hemorrhage."

38. Günner eventually returned to the United States and established himself in Dallas, Texas, where he died a few years ago.

Index

Index

Aguirre, Manuel García, Minister of Justice, 129, 130, 139, 150, 169, 182

Almonte, Gen. Juan N., 19, 24–25, 48, 79–80, 81, 87, 88, 91–92, 214; Minister to France, 25, 71; fails to sway Napoleon, 80

Arteaga, General, 46–47; executed under "Black Decree," 63, 222

Austrian Hussars, 3–4, 7, 9, 54, 67, 73–74, 114, 129, 130, 137–138, 159, 161, 219. *See also* Kevenhüller

—— troops, 11, 15, 19–20, 44, 55, 59, 81, 85. *See also* Thun; Kodolich

Barrio, Marquis Felipe Neri del, 26, 83, 93, 95, 97, 102, 103, 106, 108, 109

——, Doña Manuela Gutiérrez Estrada del, 26, 83, 93, 95, 97–98, 99, 101, 102, 103, 104, 105, 109; accompanies Carlota to Europe, 83–109

Basch, Dr. Samuel, vii, 113, 115, 129, 130, 139, 142, 145, 147, 156, 157, 159, 161, 166, 167, 169–170, 172–173, 176, 178, 179, 180, 181, 186, 198, 202–203; describes Maximilian's body after execution, 227

Bazaine, François Achille, Marshal, v, x–xi, 4, 11, 36–37, 41, 47, 48, 59, 60–61, 81, 85, 121, 127, 216, 220; marriage, 29–30; strained relations with Maximilian, 11, 45, 78, 86–87, 123–124; withdraws French troops, 45, 70–71, 79, 125–127; son born, 78; evacuates Mexico City, 125; offers to wait to escort Maximilian from country, 126; leaves Vera Cruz, 126

Belgian mission, attacked by bandits, 71–72

—— troops, 44, 59, 85, 183; in Michoacán, 45–47; prisoners, 63–64, 181. *See also* Van der Smissen

Billimeck, Professor, 68, 69–70, 113, 115, 122, 173

"Black Decree," xi, 60–63

Blasio, José Luis, petitions Maximilian to spare brother's life, 4–5; enters Emperor's service, 5–6; first contact with Emperor, 6; joins Emperor at Orizaba, 7–8; becomes secretary, 12–13; suspects estrangement between Maximilian and Carlota, 16–17; Shaffer jealous of, 28–29; persuades Dr. Lucio to treat Emperor, 72–73; leaves for Europe, 87; at Miramar, 91–94; at Rome, 97–104; returns to Mexico, 109; accompanies Maximilian to Querétaro, 129–135; with Emperor when captured, 164; bids Maximilian farewell, 177; goes to Vienna, 182–183; interview with Franz Joseph, 183–184; interviews with Archduchess Sophia, 184–185; receives only part of legacy from Maximilian's estate, 188; receives portrait of Maximilian from Carlota, 187; Maximilian's funeral, 186–187; sees Carlota at Laeken, viii, 188

Bombelles, Count Karl von, commander Palace Guard, 17, 25, 83, 87, 114, 186, 187–188

Bouslaveck, Doctor, 83, 93, 94, 95, 97, 102, 103, 104, 105, 106, 113, 114

Campbell, United States Minister to Mexico, 225

Carlota Amalia, Empress of Mexico, v–ix, xviii, 3–5, 45–46, 47, 78, 86, 114, 187–188, 215, 224; per-